LIVE SHOT
HOTSHOT

Live Shot Hot Shot — Copyright © Wayne Garcia, 2024

Wayne Garcia Consulting
Portland, OR

Paperback ISBN: 979-8-9906899-0-9
eBook ISBN: 979-8-9906899-1-6

Library of Congress Control Number: 2024909720

Garcia, Wayne
Live Shot Hot Shot/Wayne Garcia

Cover design: Tim Barber, DissectDesigns.com
Interior design by: Danielle H. Acee, AuthorsAssistant.com

Printed in the United States of America
Publisher's Cataloging-in-Publication data

First Edition

WAYNE GARCIA

HOW TO CRAFT YOUR STORIES AND CAREER AS A TV REPORTER

WRITTEN BY A TV REPORTER

LIVE SHOT

HOTSHOT

TABLE OF CONTENTS

First and foremost, I want to dedicate this book to my wife, Michele. Thanks for your encouragement and your help in making this idea a reality. And thanks for holding down the fort all those years when I was working nights, or called away to leave you and the girls, to cover breaking news. We have a lot of holidays and nights to catch up on.

You are my audience of one.

And thanks to all the great photographers I worked with in Fresno, Seattle, Los Angeles, Phoenix, and Portland.

You taught me so much about the news business, and life, at every one of my stops. We sometimes did amazing, important work. But we always laughed and learned something about the world we explored together. Thanks for being patient with me. I owe you everything.

FOREWORD BY MARK ALBERT

★ ★ ★ ★ ★

IT'S BEEN A QUARTER CENTURY since I graduated from the University of Southern California (USC) and embarked on my journalism career. While I'm proud to be part of the Trojan family (and a marching band alumni), in total journalistic honesty, nearly all of my professors in Los Angeles were completely forgettable. In fact, I can't remember a single thing from their classes or most of their names.

Except two.

And those two changed my life. In your hands right now, dear reader, you have the invaluable lessons from one of them.

In the late 1990's, both of them made journalism come alive in my head—and in my heart. One was Terry Anzur, an anchor at

KTLA-TV, Channel 5, in Los Angeles, and the other was Wayne Garcia, a reporter at crosstown rival KCAL-TV, Channel 9, who's the author of the book you're about to read.

Wayne (he asked us to call him that, not the more formal, customary Professor Garcia), was the rare teacher who taught you what you actually *needed* to know—not what some hundred-dollar textbook written by an ivory tower author with a doctorate in theoretical journalism (is that even a degree?) dictated. His once-a-week class at USC as an adjunct provided the practical, crucial, hands-on lessons that would set us up for success in the 'real world' of journalism. For example: to teach us how to be perceptive, inquisitive, persistent, and skeptical at news conferences, Wayne brought in an actual spokesman from a local law enforcement agency, who read a short, dry, wanting statement about an imaginary event. It was then our job to use our questions to pull out the full story for our audience. So impactful.

To teach us how to gather the essential elements of a story, Wayne made us get out of the studio and actually go do it. We had to find stories, we had to go check out a video camera (3/4" or VHS tape cassettes back then!), and get it on video. I still remember his verbal praise for a video story of mine (a "package") played for the class that showcased a mom and her child and the Los Angeles-based non-profit organization, Beyond Shelter (now PATH Beyond Shelter). He told us that moments like the ones I had in my story, including a mother holding her child's hand while sitting on a stairway, "don't just happen;" that as broadcast journalists, we have to seek out and gather engaging visuals to make the audience relate to our characters and care about them and their circumstances.

One evening, while Wayne was working the night shift at KCAL-TV, he let me job shadow him. As a student, a job shadow was the most valuable opportunity. Both of us arrived at his station not knowing what his story that evening would be, until the assignment desk handed it to him. It turned out it was a ride-along with the California Highway Patrol; just Wayne, a photojournalist, and me. The story, for that night's 9p & 10p newscasts, took a dramatic turn when the officer we were riding with got called to respond to a high-speed chase. So, along we went, 'code 3,' lightbar blazing and sirens wailing, with Wayne confessing in amazement to me in the backseat, "this never happens." Wayne got lucky that night to be able to share such dramatic video and story with the audience. And he made the most of it with his writing. I still remember the essence of his opening line: "You're onboard a CHP cruiser..." He immediately transported the viewer into the patrol car, starting with the best video first.

Wayne's essential lessons in the classroom, on the job, and on the air laid a foundation for my own journalism career and have stuck with me all these decades later. When the International Center for Journalists hired me to create a two-week news production course for journalists in Pakistan, I recreated Wayne's mock news conference for them. It was a revelatory experience for those Pakistani journalists, who strive to adopt many Western journalism standards in a culture not accustomed to Western-style transparency. Some years after that, I modified his mock news conference lesson while teaching journalists in Vietnam, another country with journalists admirably raising the quality of their craft. Wayne's demonstrative, immersive style of teaching has now touched the lives of journalists on at least three continents, living on in his former students, like me. Audiences worldwide are more informed because of him.

Here, in the pages that follow, Wayne imparts some of that hard-earned advice he's gathered over his remarkable, nearly forty-year journalism career, spanning cities, states, and eras. This is the book every journalist must read, so that we may serve our communities with trust, empathy, accuracy, and dedication. Wayne deftly weaves anecdotes, hard-learned lessons (writing for "an audience of one," how to develop sources) and a few *mea culpas* to deliver an essential primmer of journalism today. My only regret is he didn't publish this book sooner—preferably before I paid so much to USC! Whether you're a fresh-out-of-college journalism student, a seasoned veteran scribe, or a citizen wishing to know more about—and demystify—the Fourth Estate, Wayne's book will illuminate how journalists seek to write the first draft of history—not for them, but for the audience, so that they may make better decisions in their communities.

These days, with journalists being (falsely) labeled as an "enemy of the American people," or "sick," Wayne's lessons of how rigorous we journalists must take our responsibility remind us that such defamatory nicknames could not be further from the truth. Journalists are our neighbors, our colleagues, our fellow volunteers and charity workers; they are members of the community and care deeply about it. And it's the only private profession guaranteed in the U.S. Constitution.

Thomas Jefferson, one of the Founding Fathers of the United States of America, thought deeply about the role of a free press in the future Republic and, fortunately for us, put pen to paper to memorialize it. In 1787, two years before the ratification of the Constitution, Jefferson wrote:

> *"...were it left to me to decide whether we should have a government without newspapers or newspapers without a government, I should not hesitate a moment to prefer the latter."*

In 1799, Jefferson expanded on the essential nature of independent journalism to a free society, by writing:

> *"Our citizens may be deceived for awhile, and have been deceived;* ***but as long as the presses can be protected, we may trust to them for light."***

As journalists, it's our responsibility to uphold Jefferson's charge to us: to seek the light, without fear or favor, entrusted to keep our communities informed so that they may make reasoned decisions in governance. It would be impossible to do that without journalists like Wayne Garcia teaching us how.

Long after I took Wayne's college course, I became an on-air correspondent at CBS News, reporting across the United States and from Australia, Peru, and Taiwan. Then I created a news startup overseeing a dozen contributors, and after a bit, launched and led Hearst Television's first national investigative unit, carrying on the legacy of the storied Hearst brand. None of those opportunities would have been possible without Wayne's lessons and mentorship back at USC.

This book, *Live Shot Hotshot*, should be every journalist's first stop and an indispensable guide for anyone who wants a booster-shot of media know-how. For Professor Garcia, class is back in session.

Lucky us.

Mark Albert
Peabody Award-winning investigative journalist
CBS News, Hearst Television, Northwestern University,
Media Advisory Experts

Growth is thirty percent good advice and seventy percent being ready to hear it.
—Wayne Garcia, 2023

INTRODUCTION

CONGRATULATIONS! You are interested in, already studying about, or presently working in the field of television broadcast journalism. It is an incredibly exciting career! But I don't have to sell you on that or else why would you be reading this book? And let me tell you, we have a lot to talk about.

Before we get started, I want to share a bit about who I am, what this book is about, who this book is for, and also what makes me feel qualified to write it. I hope it will outlast the many technological changes on the horizon and will serve as an enduring TV reporter handbook.

My name is Wayne Garcia, and I've been a reporter, anchor, or manager in television news for more than thirty years. I started in radio in 1979, but my first paid TV job was in 1987 in Fresno (then Market #56) where I worked at the CBS affiliate. I started as a general assignment (GA) reporter and eventually became the weeknight anchor. From there, I moved to KIRO-TV in Seattle (Market #12) where I started again as a GA reporter and then ended up becoming a morning anchor. After three years in Seattle, I moved to Los Angeles and worked for seven years as a staff reporter in the number-two market in the country. During my time there, I covered every kind of story, including earthquakes, wildfires, mudslides, airliner crashes, Oscar parties, and the O.J. Simpson trial. I have written thousands of stories and performed even more live shots throughout the course of my career.

The bosses at KCAL didn't see me as an anchor, but that was something I wanted to pursue, so I stepped back in market size and became a weekend anchor in Phoenix (Market #11), then eventually became a primary anchor in Portland, Oregon (Market #22), and spent the bulk of my career there covering stories mostly from the desk, but also occasionally reporting from the field.

During my last year in Portland, I transitioned to assistant news director with the primary responsibility of mentoring our reporters, multimedia journalists (MMJs), and anchors. I managed about thirty people directly. It was an incredibly valuable experience that gave me great insight into where our younger journalists are excelling and where they are also struggling. A whole new generation of journalists are right now entering the workforce, and in some ways they are much better prepared than I ever was—and getting jobs in much bigger markets than I ever thought possible. But in other areas, they are falling short. And that is partly the reason I'm writing this book. I truly and sincerely want to help.

So after leaving the day-to-day business of news, I've decided to kick off my new career as a consultant and writer by sitting down at the computer and creating this book. My goal is to pass on as much as I can about what I've learned as an award-winning reporter and journalism teacher (USC 1998–2000). This business has been good to me, and I want to give back to the profession and the people embarking on a new career. I want you to know right off the bat that I don't think I'm smarter than you, but I almost certainly have more experience. I know you will benefit greatly from the lessons I've already learned. It's information that will improve your writing, interviewing, and all the other work required to get a good story on the air. In this book, you'll find proven job strategies, an understanding of what your bosses really want from you, and even how to get along with coworkers. I'm also going to teach you how to work smarter, since I know how pressed you are for time every day.

Who is this book for? If you are a journalism student in college, or even in high school, this book is for you. If you're in your first few years of working as a reporter or MMJ at a broadcast station or website or media company, this book is for you. If you are a reporter but really want to get to the anchor desk, these techniques will help. Even if you've been in the business for twenty years, I still think you'll find this book interesting and will probably relate to my experiences. If you're pursuing a career in, or already working as a public or media relations specialist, this book will help you understand what reporters want from you and how to better serve them.

I want you to take whatever you need from this book. It's fine if you disagree with some of my points. This isn't a book about journalism or ethics. My intention is that it serves as a reference guide for reporters and MMJs seeking the best ways to get good, factual, and interesting stories on the air. My advice comes not from a classroom or lecture hall but from the real world, and I've included information and examples about how real working reporters do their jobs. Some of you may find me too "old school," while others may think I'm not "Big J" enough. That's fine. But I do hope that even if you disagree with me about something, I will, at minimum, get you thinking. All I ask is that you give me a chance, and if you do, I will make you better.

I've written this book like I talk. I think it's the way you should also write for TV. So forgive my plainspokenness and incomplete sentences. It's okay. My intent is to be very approachable. We're not going to get into a whole lot of theory here. I want this book to be practical with tips you can use throughout your career. Keep this book close and refer to it when problems come up. I've got you.

So, think of me as your mentor and guide as we explore the jobs of a news reporter and MMJ. We'll cover everything from story meetings to gathering interviews to stand-ups to live shots and even how to get that first or next job. Thinking about getting an agent? I'll give you my best advice and **concrete, tangible techniques you can use right away.**

Now buckle up, relax, and get ready to explore reporting from my perspective. Before you know it, you'll be a Live Shot Hotshot and, more importantly, a solid television news reporter!

Just remember, it's only news.

THE JOB/YOUR DAY

I'M GOING TO TELL YOU SOMETHING I want you to never forget. Your job is extremely simple—not easy, but simple. It's not brain surgery. When you are confused, down, not sure what to do or where to go, frantic from extreme deadline pressure, trying to write your story in ten minutes with producers and others breathing down your neck, remember: **your job is to communicate one simple story to one person.** That's it. Everything you do throughout your day—the driving, phone calls, texts, emails, discussions with your bosses and producers and coworkers—all comes down to the finished product. And even though your story will be seen by hundreds or thousands of people, it's not the same as if you were on a big screen at a football stadium. People don't usually watch news in groups. Your story should be created for what I call the "audience of one."

So who is this person? Who is your audience of one? That's a great question. I'm glad I asked it. When I was first starting in the business, I envisioned my parents as my target audience. They were TV news viewers, they were relatable to me, and I could envision them watching my story and anticipate any questions or criticisms they would have. Later, my target audience was my wife. And as I wrote, I'd imagine her over my shoulder saying, "Hey, what does that mean?" Or "Wow, do you think you're being fair to that guy? Just because he wouldn't talk to you, isn't there something you could say to illustrate his position?"

It was a big help to me being able to get outside of my own head whenever I would write, to imagine how the audience would react, and what questions they'd have. Would they have any reason to think my story wasn't hitting the right tone or wasn't respectful? And I think this technique will work for you. (We'll explore further in the writing section of this book.)

For now, though, in your mind, create a target viewer that you relate to and already have a relationship with, and that is the person to always consider when creating your story. They're your audience of one (or two) who hover over your interviews, scriptwriting, and live shots. Think of people you respect—who you would never lie, exaggerate, or talk down to. Instead, it should be someone you are comfortable talking with! Tell that target audience (your personal audience) the most important part of what you've learned that day. After all, you're really doing your job for them. To me, journalism is all about investigating and seeking out the truth then reporting back to the people who don't have the time or know-how to do it themselves.

Now, let's talk about your day and how the rest of this book is laid out. If you're fortunate to work dayside, you'll need to get to work around nine or ten a.m. That's usually when the story meetings that will decide your fate for the day take place. From there, it's all about fine-tuning the angle of your story and arranging interviews. Then it's time to actually leave the safety of the building and head out into the real world, with or without a photographer. Then you must shoot interviews, shoot video of your subject (B-roll), maybe do a stand-up, and hopefully grab a bite to eat. During your morning, if you know your story is coming together, this would also be a good time to post on social media what you're covering and what you've found. Just be careful not to tip your hand to the competition. If things aren't working out, you'll want to let the station know as soon as possible so you can work together to figure out alternatives. Because, as you will find out, not being on the air and turning a story is not an option for you.

Assuming all is going well, there will soon be time for you to log your video (look at everything you or the photographer shot), transcribe the interview (or not), and begin to write your story.

Hopefully, at least ninety minutes before your story airs, you'll be finished writing the story and ready to record your voice track. Then it's time to edit, set up the live shot, and go present your story for the newscast.

But you're not quite done yet. You might have to break down your story for later newscasts or even go live again with a new or updated version of your story.

Then it's finally time for you to head back to the station, perhaps write a version of your story for the web, put away your gear, and, finally, write an end-of-shift (EOS) note to tell the newsroom what you did and who you talked to, leaving contact numbers, information, and other angles to pursue if you didn't get to all of them.

Wow! That day had a lot packed into it, and the time went by so fast. Didn't you wish you could have extended your day by just twenty minutes to give you a little more time to write or edit? It's always that way, and that's part of what's so great about our jobs. In other industries, most look at their watch or the clock just hoping the hands will move faster so they can go home. In the TV news biz, when you look at your watch or phone late in the day you just pray time would just slow down a little. There's always more you wish you could include. "My story would be so much better if I just had a little more time." But you never do. That's just the way it is.

So do your best with the time you have. Don't try to be perfect, and NEVER miss your slot. Be safe, though. Never risk an accident or ticket. Get what you can done on time, even if it's a little rough, because there's always tomorrow.

That leads me to my last point before we get into the meat of the book: How to handle criticism from external sources *and* yourself. Remember to give yourself a break. The really great thing about news is that we start fresh every day. Even if you miss something, or blow your live shot, don't dwell on it. Learn from it, yes, but don't beat yourself up over it. We're all human. If we didn't get it perfect today, or even if you did a crazy-good job today, it doesn't matter after you go home. Because tomorrow you'll have to prove yourself all over again. That's life in the TV news world.

I always liked that aspect about it, and it helped keep me grounded. If I knocked it out of the park, I never got too full of myself. If I blew it on a story, I never got too down. News life is a marathon, not a sprint. And if you live or die each day by how good your story was, you'll be miserable and won't last long. Learn, grow, move on.

That advice goes double for the criticism you will face from bosses, viewers, and others throughout your career. There will be mean phone calls, horrible emails, and snide social media posts about you. Once in a while, the criticism directed at you will be thoughtful, constructive, and appropriate. But it's still tough to hear. My best advice is that when someone says something negative about you, don't react immediately. Think about it (for a day or a week). Then, if you think they have a point, and be really honest with yourself about that, try to incorporate their suggestions.

I'm not talking about factual errors here that need to be corrected immediately. I'm speaking about comments people offer you about your approach, your choice of clothing, or the tone of your story. If people are just downright mean and rude, **don't respond**. That will really get them. They want you to engage. Don't do it, and don't ever repost their comments, giving them the power and punch of *your* social media. It just gives them more air, and you can never win those arguments, trust me. Just ignore them and forget about it after you block them—easier said than done, I know. Of course, there are always exceptions. If you are threatened or feel unsafe, report that to your news director right away.

I can't tell you how many times that I've seen a reporter get thirty comments on social media about a story. Twenty-nine are positive or engaging. One is horribly negative. Guess which one the reporter responds to? Yep. It's human nature. But resist the urge. You'll be way better off hitting the block button and moving on.

There has been a negative perception of TV journalists in recent years (e.g., "fake news"). And sometimes, we face hostility from all sides. Unfortunately, some of the reasons for that perception are justified and have been earned by those who are not genuine journalists. Journalists should strive to be truthful, fair, honest, and unbiased. And it's hard for viewers to think of us all as trustworthy. Many just see the camera and microphone and assume we're all the same. In my experience, the people I've worked with have always strived to be fair, accurate, and transparent. And I know you will, too. That should always be the goal.

Sometimes our jobs can be downright dangerous. But with all that facing us, don't forget what a truly special, exciting job this is! We are paid to get a front-row seat to history every day. We are creators. We go out into the community and see and meet people every single day, then we use our tools and our brains to create audio/visual stories to serve as a record of what happened. We have a lot of freedom in the field. We decide who to interview, what questions to ask, where to go to get our story, how to write it, what shots to put in when we edit it, and finally how to present it. We learn to listen to our gut or our "news nose." We work to find the real story, not just the one assigned to us. We don't sit behind a desk all day. Time goes by so fast. And at the end of the day, we get to be part of a show—a news program where we can show and tell the community, city, country, or world what WE discovered.

We write history in real time. There's no other job like it. If it's in your blood, your heartbeat has probably increased a couple of beats per minute just reading this. Now let's figure out how to do all those things I just told you about.

THE STORY MEETING

"OKAY, SO WHO HERE HAS A STORY IDEA?"

I think most every story meeting I've ever attended in my long news career has begun with that question. Sometimes there are reporters waiting in line to give producers and assignment desk staffers their best pitches on one or two ideas they've vetted and are prepared to cover that day.

But most days, well, there is silence. And that silence is the crashing sound of opportunity for you...big opportunity. I will soon explain why the morning (or afternoon meeting for nightsiders) is so important for you to make your mark in the newsroom. But let's back up.

What is the story meeting or assignment meeting all about? Why do we need it? Who runs it? How can I get noticed there, and why should I want to stand out?

Let's begin. The story meeting is where producers, the architects of the newscast, and the assignment desk, which tracks the multitude of *possible* stories out there, come together. They are joined by the reporters, MMJs, and sometimes photographers, who will actually be the ones going out to do those stories. Also in attendance will most likely be someone from the web staff, one or two managers, an executive producer or assistant news director, and just maybe the News Director. I have worked in some newsrooms where reporters weren't required to sit in the story meeting. I've been in others where attendance was very much required. If it's an option at your station, make sure you get there on time or even a few minutes early. If it's a requirement, definitely be there on time and ready to work.

What you need to understand is that **this is your opportunity to get some rare face time in front of all those folks.** Think about it. You're out in the field ninety percent of your day. But in this meeting, they get to see you as a person (in person). They learn personal tidbits about you, see your personality off camera, and can form their opinion about what kind of worker you are. You want to be the person who stands out by being there on time and coming to the meeting armed with ideas. Also, bring along a positive attitude. This is huge. Instead of telling people why a story can't be done, think about what you'll need to successfully do the story and ask for that instead. Offer input on other reporters' stories (without being pushy). Speak up if you have a contact in the community that might help another reporter. Be present and engaged!

Another reason why you want to be there, take part, and offer ideas is that in many cases, you are deciding your own fate for the day. If I had a reporter come in excited about a story, as long as it was a hard news story, we'd almost always approve that assignment. You want to know who always got the least-favorite and hardest story to turn for the day? The person who showed up late without ideas—every time.

A lot of decisions are made during those twenty- or thirty-minute story meetings (they should never be longer than that). Assignment editors offer up a list of the potential stories, and producers and other managers then decide what stories they care the most about and want to assign to a reporter or MMJ. It's a numbers game. On any given day, there may be ten stories worth covering, but you may only have up to five reporters who work that shift. There's not enough staff to cover everything. So judgments need to be made about what stories reporters/MMJs will cover. Occasionally, though, there are more reporters than stories. On those days, you absolutely want to have some good ideas to pitch.

The factors that go into the decisions about where to assign crews are many and include practicality.

- **WHAT CAN ACTUALLY BE TURNED?** In other words, the group may like a story, but it's two hours away, so it's not likely a reporter can get there in time to cover it. Other stories may be too complex or controversial for a day turn, and time may be needed to begin advance work on them. So a story that can positively be turned the same day is needed. In other words, if you are sent out, you will definitely come back with that story.

- **WHAT STORY FITS THE STATION'S BRAND OR NEWSCAST?** This can vary widely within a market. Is your station the one that is constantly monitoring city government, or does it lead with crime? Maybe homelessness is something your news managers have determined through research that viewers care most about. If so, you can bet that at least one of your station's stories will be about that issue. Your job as a reporter at your station is to quickly figure out what kinds of stories have great appeal and then try to find stories to pitch to fit that niche. Sometimes you can push managers and producers to cover a story you care about that doesn't quite fit the station identity, but you have to build up some goodwill first. And you do that by going out and reliably turning the stories that are important to your producers and managers. I'm not saying this is the ideal way to cover news, but it's a reality, and you'll find almost all newsrooms work this way.

Before we launch into any more information about how to create stories for our station and for our viewers, let's address a few basics about news itself. For starters, what is news? It seems like such a basic question, but I bet the answers you get from other journalists and from your target audience will vary greatly. Let's face it, without viewers we don't have jobs, so your target audience's opinion should carry considerable weight. In the end, if we only covered the stories that journalists think are important, we'd be broadcasting to a very small audience and eventually we'd all be out looking for work.

So, again, what is news? Over the course of my career, I've had a long time to think about that question, and here's what I've come up with. I'm sure over time you'll develop your own ideas. But my definition of news contains three parts.

1. **NEWS SHOULD BE NEW!** Hey, that was easy. I mean, the word "new" is in it. So the first component of news should be something that happened recently—a bus crash, a just passed law, or a grand opening. Remember coming home from school and your parents asking you, "What's new? What happened in school today?" Everyone wants to hear what's new. We all want to know what just changed in our world. So every story you do should have some newness to it, or it's your job to find the newness in it.

2. **NEWS SHOULD BE IMPORTANT, RELEVANT.** It should be about something that we all need to know that has the potential of changing or altering our lives, like an impending winter snowstorm. In fact, news managers have learned just how important weather is to viewers, and that's why you see so much of it in newscasts.

3. **NEWS SHOULD BE INTERESTING.** There should be something about the story that catches our attention, intrigues us, or makes us want to watch. Think about coming

home from school again. The thing you want to tell your parents and the thing they most want to hear is the most interesting thing that happened to you that day. When you're on a date, you want to share interesting things across the dinner table. You want to hear interesting things in return. It's in our nature.

But, unfortunately, we live in the real world, and few stories in ANY newscast meet all three parts of my definition. Heck, sometimes there are stories that have none of the three assets. That's the reality of having to fill so much time with limited staff we all deal with, from New York City to Bismarck. We could always use more writers, producers, and reporters. The reason I explained my definition of news is so that you can understand and begin to develop news judgment. You can help determine which stories are more valuable in your newscast and which can be eliminated. More than that, now that you know the definition, you can work harder to make sure the stories that you turn for the newscast include newness, importance, and interest. That's the goal. It won't happen every day, but there's always something new in the story, you just have to find it. Why is it important? Important to whom? Explain why. And for gosh sakes, make the story interesting and something people will pay attention to by finding characters, using great video and natural sound, and throwing in surprises, which we'll talk more about later.

EXCAVATING STORY IDEAS

Coming up with story ideas doesn't happen overnight. It's something you need to work at all the time. One of the things I like best about TV news is that there's really no homework. You do the best you can that day and then you start fresh the next. That's mostly true, but there is one part of the job that requires you to be "on" all the time—finding story ideas. Keep your eyes and ears open. Sometimes the best ideas come from where you get your hair cut or at the gym. What are people talking about? What interests them? Those are two of the three aspects you need for a good story right there—new and interesting. Whether it's important or not, you can figure out later. Here are some ways to discover story ideas.

1. PAY ATTENTION TO YOUR SURROUNDINGS.

A chain store where you're shopping posts a sign that they are closing. That could be a great story. A sign asking for donations at the donut shop to help a woman recover from a fire could be a story. Your bank tells you they can't give you more than ten, one-dollar bills because there's a shortage could be a story. Stories are all around us. Listen, pay attention, and write down your ideas on your phone notes app or an old-fashioned notepad. Find a system that works. Then investigate or "vet" them to see if they hold your interest.

Speak up in the meeting and say, "Hey, I was outside my gym the other day, and they had this robot patrolling the parking lot because there have been a bunch of break-ins. I talked to the manager, and he said we could go out and see how it works." That right there is a great story pitch. You've found something interesting *and* made some inquiries about it, showing you can actually turn the story if it is assigned to you. If you've worked on an idea at all, and you're confident you can cover it well, *pitch it.* There have been many times I've kicked myself because I've seen or heard something and thought, *That's interesting,* but didn't write it down or tell anyone. Then guess what? I see it on the competition's broadcast later in the week.

2. ADVANCE STORY IDEAS FROM THE COMPETITION.

We all do it. A story you hear on the radio, see on a newspaper's website, or even a story done by another TV station can be used in a pinch. Maybe a station in another city has broken a story about a subject that also affects your market. Believe me, stations aren't above copying each other. But it's best to not rely on that method. You don't want to be the person in the morning meeting saying, "Hey, I saw this great story last night on Channel 5. We should do that too." Still, it's a good idea to have a list of websites to check every morning that may give you thought starters.

Independent news sites, sites that serve a specific niche such as cycling, hiking, fishing, etc. can sometimes offer great ideas. Just to be clear, you should never copy those stories and claim them as your own. But you could use an article or post as a thought starter and do your own research and interviews to write your own story, which may not even turn out the same as the article that gave you the idea.

The way to pitch a story from the competition: "Hey, I saw this great story on Channel 5 last night, and I did some research this morning and found out it's not only happening in Merced. Madera just passed a city ordinance about it, and they've got a victim who has given us permission to use his video and will talk to us about the scam."

Just know that sometimes the competition will do such a great job on a story that there is no way you can independently verify it. In those cases, if it's a story your station has to have, you absolutely need to tell your viewers where you got the story, giving credit to the original author and source.

3. DEVELOP SOURCES.

The best way I've found to generate story ideas is to develop relationships with people who work in places like the Mayor's office, the police or fire department, the courts, downtown associations, community organizations, etc. These are the people who can alert you to great story ideas that you could be the first to break (and be a shining hero in your newsroom). However, developing these relationships takes a while. You must cultivate trust with people "on the inside" so they know you won't burn them as a source. They can give you a tip, but that is only a starting point. You need to do your own research and investigating to confirm the tip and get people to speak with you on the record, or find documents that support the tip.

The only way to cultivate these incredibly valuable sources, is to GET OUT in the community and meet people. Be curious. Volunteer, have coffee in different parts of the city, ask to do ride-alongs with police and fire departments. Spend time getting to know people who run homeless shelters and youth centers in different parts of the city. Ask them questions. Give them your number. You can also build sources just from the stories you do every day. Always leave a card with the people you interview and tell them to call you if they ever have a good story idea.

Many times, your source won't want to be identified for fear of losing their job, and you'll need to protect their identity. Remember, you're not doing a story on the information they are providing; you are using their information as a starting point to do your own research about the story. For example, a source at the police department tells you, "Hey, guess what? Our Chief of Police was arrested last night in Porterville after speaking at an out-of-town fundraiser. He had too many Coors Lights, and an officer pulled him over leaving town on Highway 65." That tip allows you to check with the Porterville Police Department.

"Hey, guys, this is Wayne Garcia from Channel 58. I got a tip that you guys busted a neighboring town's police chief, John Smith. Is that true?"

Or, if you have a source in said police department, you might want to ask that person if it's true to get more information to make an official inquiry. But never out your sources, and only use them to *begin* investigations. I never revealed sources, even to my own station. They didn't care as long as I could then provide the proof (such as court documents) that the tip led to a bona fide story.

Let's bottom-line it now. The great news for you is that it doesn't take much to stand out from the crowd in your newsroom. Get there on time, have a positive attitude, tackle any story with a smile on your face, do your best, come with ideas, remember what constitutes "news," and work hard at developing sources. This model will set you up for incredible success.

And we're only just getting started. Let's move on to what you need to do once you get your assignment.

GATHERING

I WOULDN'T SAY THIS IS THE MOST IMPORTANT PART OF YOUR DAY, all parts are important. But let's just say if you don't get this right, it sets a limit on how good the rest of your day and your story will turn out. "Gathering" is my word for what you do once you leave the story meeting—the thinking, plotting, planning, phone calls, emails, research, and actions you'll take over the next four or so hours to assemble all the raw materials you'll need for your story. I guess you could call it hunting too because you will be hunting down interviews, information, source cooperation, and many other things that rarely ever fall into your lap.

You might be wondering how I came up with the four-hour time period for gathering all your shots and interviews. Here's how: If you start your day at 10 a.m., chances are you won't be finished with the morning meeting, your coffee, and greeting the folks in the newsroom until 11 a.m. If you're the lead at 4 p.m., that gives you five hours until showtime. But you have to subtract writing time, editing time, and feeding time. That's an hour at minimum, more like two. So you really need to be done shooting by 2 p.m. if you're in the 4 p.m. show, or 3 p.m. if you're in the 5 p.m. show. So you have about four hours at most to gather all the elements for your story on an average day, which goes by really, really, fast. So say your hellos and goodbyes quickly and get out the door! You will need those precious minutes later in the day. Oh, and that four hours also includes driving time, so you'd better get out the door because it's already 10:40 a.m. and you're the lead at 4 p.m.

Once you are handed your assignment and are clear on the angle or angles that are being envisioned by your producers and bosses, the ball is in your court. Keep in mind, the story you find is often NOT what people in the meeting thought it would be. I'll say that again. The story that is discussed in the meeting is rarely the exact story you'll find in the field. Viewer tips can be wrong or some-what inaccurate. Press releases promising great video sometimes fudge the truth to get you to show up. Events can be canceled. People are flaky and decide they don't want to be on the news after all. Or, sometimes, when you get out to the story, you'll find an even better one than the original pitch! All of those cases are fine.

Don't make up any story to suit your bosses. Don't fudge, don't lie. NEVER invent information! Do the story that's really out there, but make sure you keep in touch and communicate with folks back at the station so there are no surprises for them as they tease your story or plan additional coverage around it.

A recent example: We did a story on a restaurant that closed in a once-popular area of town. It was a chain restaurant, and the fact it was closing really was a symptom of decay in that particular area. When the reporter got to the restaurant, she found a note on the door announcing the closure but there was no one there—no customers, no workers, no one nearby—it was a bit isolated.

What to do? I suggested that she try going to the only nearby restaurant that *was* still open. What was their secret? What did they think of all the nearby closures? Luckily, it was an independent restaurant that didn't have to ask for corporate approval to talk to the media, and she got some great sound. They were busier than ever but also sad to see the decay of the area. This is an example of not doing the story we had envisioned but still turning a good story on the issue. And the reporter was able to contrast the closed restaurant and empty parking lot to the bustling activity at the other restaurant.

Contrasts are always great for storytelling and editing! Plus, it reinforced a great lesson I learned in this career: When you're trying to do a story on something and it's not working, look for the opposite angle. If it's dead where you are, where is it busy and why? If it's dirty here, where is it clean? If this area is dangerous, which area is really safe? Think outside the box.

Back to your day. Over the next few hours, you know you'll have to find interviews, b-roll, and outside sources such as supporting documents, surveillance videos, or photos. You need to send out clearance forms if you're going to use outside video and get permission so you don't get sued. Then sift through all the important facts you've gathered and determine which ones you absolutely need to include in the story and which ones aren't as important— also which facts you don't understand or need clarity on. You may need help making graphics or maps for your story. But in order to get those in time, you need to start asking for that help now, and be specific about what you want. There will never be enough time or room for everything, trust me.

I'm going to take you back in time now, to Fresno, California, circa 1989. I had been in the TV biz for two years already, but every day at the gathering stage I'd be slightly panicked. This was always the worst part of my day. Even with two years under my belt, I wasn't ever confident that I'd be able to turn a package in the time allotted. There's a lot to do and very little time to do it. Where to start? It was too much...**overwhelming!**

What eventually helped me be more confident was realizing what I really needed to turn a story on any given day. Here's a little secret: I like to solve problems by going to the end and working my way backward. You ever notice how it's easier to solve a maze when you start at the end and work back to the starting point? Life is a lot like that. Picture exactly what you want, then work backward to figure out how to get it. When I imagine what I want for dinner, I picture the dinner plate and everything on it until in my mind it's exactly right, then I go get the ingredients and make it. And this same approach helped me with crafting news stories. When I was finally able to pin down the most basic ingredients of a "story recipe," I was calm.

Most local news stories these days run between 1:30 (minutes and seconds) and 1:45 in length. At least, that's the goal, even if reporters always seem to go over. If I'm shooting for a story that is 1:30 in length, I know from experience that's basically three short sound bites and three or four short tracks (the parts the reporter writes and voices). And when you look at it that way, it doesn't seem so hard. Three bites, three or four short tracks. A track is only three sentences at most. Add in some natural sound, and you're golden. Feel calmer? Now it's time to gather.

The first thing to do is understand the raw basics of the story that you're assigned. Most times there are past articles, file video, and other notes that will help guide you. So you should quickly scan any notes and start thinking about who you need to interview. The goal is to interview someone who is affected by the story in some way and has an opinion about the story.

Sometimes you're assigned a story that involves a press conference. That's good and bad. Good because interviews are already lined up, and all you need to do is point the microphone and camera in the right direction. But also bad because I don't believe you should just rely on press conference video or interviews. Most of the time, if the story only includes a government official, that makes for a very boring and dry story. There are always exceptions. A press conference involving the family of someone recently released from prison will probably be interesting.

Plus, from a press conference, you may be getting the people who are creating the action of your story but probably not the people who are actually affected by that action. Frankly, to me, the press conference would be the least important part of my story. Let's use a made-up example to illustrate the point:

Your story is about a city park that is reopening today after being closed for months because of drug use and vandalism. Now police have a better handle on crime, city work crews have installed new benches and playground equipment, and the mayor will be cutting the ribbon on the park at 11 a.m.

What you probably are figuring out is that just getting the mayor and other city dignitaries opening up the park isn't enough. It's the start of the story but not the story itself. I would look for people who live, work, or travel around that park to get *their* perspective on what the park reopening means.

I believe you should mostly try to minimize coverage of officials and instead focus on "real" people. This has been a very important part of the way I approach stories, and I believe it's what made them more relevant to our viewers than just relying on official sound bites. I value including "real" people in my stories over officials because they have the most at stake in any situation, are probably least politically motivated, the most candid, and, let's face it, they are more interesting.

We know the mayor isn't going to say anything earthshaking or surprising. She's going to thank a bunch of people and talk about how good a job they are doing. I might want a short bite from the mayor, or sound of the ribbon cutting, but I'd be more interested in the people who came out to watch. What do they think? And I'd wonder if maybe we could tell the entire story through their eyes. Someone who lives there may have a heartwarming story of what this really means in their daily life. Or they may be able to share a terrible story of what it used to be like. Or maybe they have serious doubts that the park will be able to stay a safe place.

There are always exceptions. If you're in breaking news, trying to figure out how fast a fire is moving and where it's going, or trying to find out how strong an earthquake was, it's fine to use officials, in fact it's a must. But in most cases, I've found that officials/ politicians provide the base of the story, and the real meat comes from talking with "real" people.

So how do you find them? There is no substitute for getting out of the station and doing the hard work of walking around the neighborhood and talking to people. Google the name of the park and see if there are any interesting stories that pop up such as a past crime there. Or maybe the park is named after someone whose relatives are still alive. What do they think? These past stories can be leads to new angles that you might want to use today. Walk around, knock on doors, go up to people and strike up a conversation. Talk to the mom and kids on the swing. We'll go into this more in "The Interview" chapter.

Whether you're alone or fortunate enough to work with a pho- tographer, the car ride to the story is a great time to discuss (or go over in your mind) how you're going to make the story come together. What shots will you need? In our park example, you'll need shots of the park, people playing in it, hopefully, maybe file video of the park at its worst, and interviews with people who have a stake in the park or care about it. When you get to the park, you'll look for all those opportunities. You'll also need natural sound, which is very important.

When I was working as a reporter, I would always chat with my photographer on the way to a story about what I knew about the story and what I'd expect to find there. Some photographers are more interested than others. But when you get one who really wants to do a great job, the back and forth is really fun. And I would go through this exercise with them:

"Okay, how is everyone else going to do this story?" After they replied with their guesses, I'd ask, "So how can we make it different?" And then we'd imagine other angles we could take and situations to watch out for. We'd throw out wacky, crazy ideas, which we mostly threw out, but sometimes they made sense to try. But you never know what you can do until you get out there, which is why it's important to never write the story before you see what's happening. But it's also critical to be prepared and be organized in your approach. I think pushing yourself to find the unexpected, the twist, the surprise in every story you do is what will make your stories stand out. And they'll be more interesting to the viewer. Never settle for being spoon-fed a story. There is almost always gold to be found out there that will make your stories rise and shine above the competition.

That's a real setback facing MMJs: They just don't have another person to bounce ideas off of. But maybe you have a manager, anchor, fellow MMJ, or reporter who has expressed a willingness to help, and you can call and chat with that person on the way. If you're stumped, just the act of expressing the problem out loud can often result in you finding the solution.

The most important thing I can tell you is to get out of the station ASAP! Get out and drive to the location to see what you find.

Way too often, reporters stay in the station and make call after call, and the clock is ticking. If you're working with a photographer, make use of your cell phone and make those calls from out in the field. If you're by yourself, drive to the scene and make your calls from there, all the while keeping an eye out for something you might want to document or a person you might like to interview. Just the act of getting the camera out of the car and placing it on a tripod and standing next to it will *many* times motivate people to come up to you, curious about what you're doing. This is a golden opportunity to gather information and interviews.

Three bites, four tracks at a minimum. Get that first. Then if you have time, see what else you can find. Make sure you have the video to cover the words you're going to write. Get natural sound. Be focused. Be organized. Ask questions if you don't understand something. Gather your elements while always remembering what you want to say and what angle you think tells the story the best. You don't have to tell the whole story. Just tell the most interesting part. Say less, but make every word you write count.

When are you finished gathering? Consider the sum of what you've gathered so far versus the time you have left before you need to start editing. Some days, you get everything you need within the first hour. That's rare. Most days, you struggle to get barely enough. That's part of the reason why being focused when gathering is so important. It will make shooting, writing, and editing so much easier. Eventually, you'll be able to find your focus quickly. You'll realize you just don't have time to include everything. So which is the key part? That becomes your story. Your interview questions will be focused, and best and most important of all, your story will be understandable to the viewer.

There is one situation where you are forced to gather, write, and present all at the same time. It's called Breaking News. And that's what we're going to learn about next.

BREAKING NEWS
SPECIAL
REPORT

"Where's Wayne? Has he checked in yet? How far is he from the scene? I need him in my A block!"

"He and Jen are on the way. From where they were, it will take them a good half hour to get out there."

"A half hour? That's too long. Tell them to hurry!"

I COULDN'T EVEN GUESS how many breaking news stories I've covered in my time as a reporter in Fresno, Seattle, Los Angeles, and Phoenix. But every one of those stories was extremely important to the people back at the station. There is no denying the race to be first. And why not? It's one of the only chances you really get to see how you measure up to the competition in real time. Who's first on the air? Who's first with the "money shots?" Who can break the news first on social media? In these situations, all eyes are trained on the other stations to see who can get the live pictures on TV before anyone else.

Well, after doing this most of my adult life I'll tell you the truth. You win some, you lose some. And most of it is out of your control. But there are some important things you can do to prepare yourself to cover breaking news when you get the call. This chapter deals with what you need to know to report breaking news like a pro, including how to balance the station's immediate needs versus your safety and your duty to make sure you have enough material to tell the story after the breaking event is over.

Let's begin by addressing some fundamental questions. First, what is breaking news? *Duh,* you may think. *Everyone knows the answer to that. It's those important stories where the producers throw in this stinger music and change over the graphics to red.* But there is, or at least should be, much more that goes into the definition and the thought process. You may be surprised to know that in many of the newsrooms where I've worked, producers, managers, and anchors have had serious discussions, even arguments, over whether to brand a story as "breaking" and how long to keep that branding alive. Every station you work for should have some guidelines for you to follow, but generally, I consider breaking news to have these qualities:

- **BREAKING NEWS MUST BE IMPORTANT.** Lives or property are at risk. Or perhaps a huge legal decision has just been made that will affect lives. Someone important (well-known) has died or has had a serious accident. Or there is an important development to previous breaking news that viewers need to be alerted about.
- **BREAKING NEWS MUST BE HAPPENING NOW.** Most times this is clear cut. A fire is spreading downtown. A riot is breaking out at the prison. The mayor has just been found not guilty of murder. Immediacy is a key component of breaking news. It is literally the "breaking" part of the two-word term.
- **BREAKING NEWS SHOULD BE UNPLANNED.** You can fight me on this one. But I don't think a scheduled landing of the president's plane at the airport is breaking news. My hesitation to use the breaking news open is that the more you use breaking news branding for marginal stories, the more you water down that vital branding, and people stop paying attention to it. What I love about news is that it's not math. Different people can have different opinions, and several can be right.
- **IT'S IMPORTANT TO KNOW WHEN BREAKING NEWS IS OVER.** For most crime stories, my indicator was whether police units were still on the scene. If they were still blocking streets, had crime tape up, were gathering evidence, and/or still searching for suspects, I continued to call it "breaking." A murder that happens at 3 p.m. can be called breaking through the 6 p.m. newscast, but after that, you're not really breaking the news to your viewers anymore. Those who watch already

know. There are stories that have the staying power to be considered breaking for days. Earthquakes where there are continuing developments, including aftershocks and rescues, comes to mind. Hurricanes, states of emergency, wildfires… As long as new, important situations are still happening it's okay to still call it breaking news. But this is where newsroom guidelines and judgment come into play. Everyone will have their own philosophy, but the news director and management team have the final call. And your management team should have some clear definitions of what they consider breaking news. If they don't, ask them for guidance.

Now that we've established what breaking news is, let's move forward to discuss what breaking news means to you, the reporter and/or photographer. Let's begin with who gets called to cover breaking news. Well it won't come as a surprise to you that usually it's the crew that's closest to where the breaking news is happening. But not always. There are several factors that go through a news manager's head when assigning a crew to go to breaking news. Location is first. Second is how serious is the breaking news? If it's really serious, whoever is closest will go, period. Serious school bus accidents, high-rise fires—stories that are big and changing by the minute need to have a crew there as soon as humanly possible.

But there are other stories that classify as breaking that may allow a news manager to consider other factors about who to send. If the scene is stable and unlikely to change in the next half hour, such as a big power outage, airport shutdown, or huge traffic tie-up, the assignment desk might instead ask all the reporters or MMJs how far along they are on their original stories before deciding who to send. No one wants to lose a story, and if they send you to breaking news, they may be sacrificing your original story. The reverse is also true. Maybe you are totally striking out on your story and have next to nothing, then you would be the perfect person to send to breaking news.

Sometimes managers will ask the most capable ad-libber on the reporting staff to go cover breaking news. It might not be fair because how do you get good if you're never picked? But that's the way it is. I told you I'd be honest with you. But I'm still going to give you strategies to make you better at covering breaking news so you're ready for anything. When I was a reporter, I always liked to get my work done as soon as possible. Shoot, write, edit, and be done well before the newscast. So if there was breaking news, I could go cover it. It's also way less stressful to have your story done early.

Sometimes breaking news happens out of town (way out of town). If your station has a travel budget, you might be asked to get on a plane to go cover a wildfire or a volcano eruption in another state or even country. To be among the first to be considered, make sure you're a solid, trustworthy reporter. And make sure to have a travel bag at the station or in your car that enables you to leave on a moment's notice. You should invest in cold-weather gear and fire/hot-weather gear, and keep any needed medication with you at all times. Nothing makes a manager happier than hearing a reporter or MMJ say, "I've got my go-bag right here. I'm ready and can be at the airport in twenty minutes." They'll remember that, and your stock will rise several points just for being prepared.

But most breaking news happens close to home, so let's now talk about what is expected and how best to meet the challenge of covering breaking news when you get that frantic text or call.

Once you're notified you're being pulled for breaking, try to be careful and calm. Don't ever speed to breaking news. Don't rush. Be quick, careful, and get going, but don't race to the story. Why? Because in all the many, many, breaking stories I've covered, never once did it matter that I was there five minutes earlier. What can happen, though, is you get a speeding ticket, or worse, get in an accident on the way. Or heaven forbid, you hit someone. And guess what? That's on you, not the station. They won't pay your ticket and may fire you for being in an accident. So just be quick and careful but never reckless. It's all a crapshoot anyway. Many times I've gotten the best stuff by being first to the scene and many times I've gotten the best stuff by being last to the scene. If you're a veteran reporter reading this right now, I know you'll agree with me.

What's important in covering breaking news is to have a good memory and to notice what normally wouldn't be considered important. When anchors toss to you for a report on "what's going on out there," they expect you to give them information. But the problem is, many times when you arrive to breaking news, no one is willing to provide you any facts yet. That will not, however, stop the anchors from saying your name and taking your live shot. So it's important for you to have something to say.

So here is the first thing you need to do: Look around. Use your environment. Talk about what you see. Don't guess. *Just describe what you see.* If it's a fire or crime scene, talk about how you were able to get there. Were streets blocked off as you were navigating to the area? Was there traffic on the way? How many police or fire units do you see? If it's appropriate, mention weather conditions. Will it be extra hot for firefighters? Which way is the wind blowing if there's been a gas leak or chemical spill? Do you see a body in the street? You don't have to wait for police to tell you someone is dead if you can see a sheet covering a body with your own two eyes. What's burning? Where's the fire? Talk about your location because many viewers won't know where you are.

> *"Hey, we're here just two blocks away from Monarch High School across from Dewey Park in the northwest part of the city."*

That's a great way to communicate to viewers where the action is happening. Remember what you saw driving in. Were there crowds gathered? Which streets were impassable? Those are all nuggets you can use. Did any fire trucks make you pull over on the way? Does it seem as though units are scaling back, or are more units arriving? What does it sound like, smell like? These are all topics you can talk about without having any official facts about what's going on.

Besides getting there and setting up a live shot, make sure to actually shoot and record what you see. Hopefully, you have a photographer with you, but if you're an MMJ, this is an extremely tough situation and probably the most challenging part of your job. You need to gather information, shoot video, try to find witnesses, and prepare to go live all while communicating with the desk and producers. I frankly think it's too much for one person in many cases. But do your best.

Your safety is the number-one consideration, and you need to be your own advocate in requesting help from the station. If they can't help you, then be safe and tell them you're doing your best. Don't feel pressured. Work quickly, but don't take chances. Remember to record as much as you can for future use, including your live shots and live interviews. Chances are very good you'll have to write a story later, and it sucks trying to do that when you forgot to record because you were so busy going live. Ask me how I know? I've been there.

When covering breaking news, consider the reliability of your witnesses. You have to be very careful. Many times, what people told me about what happened wasn't actually true. They were either too excited to remember correctly, or they passed on hearsay as their own accounts. Witnesses are great, but you have to understand, they can only speak to what they know and feel. You need to establish what the witness actually saw with their own eyes and not just what is being said around the neighborhood. Even then you have to be careful.

When I was covering breaking news, I really tried to report only what I could see, and what officials told me. Even then sometimes the information turned out to not be fully correct. The best you can do is make sure that beyond what you can see, you attribute the information to the official, agency, or witness that gave you the information.

"Police told me they are looking for one gunman."

"A firefighter told me they are running out of oxygen for their crews and have had to pull back from inside the building."

"The store manager told me he was the one who pulled the fire alarm after smelling smoke near the storage room."

Be wary of really specific information from witnesses very early in covering breaking news! Never report names or races of victims or suspects in the minutes you begin to cover breaking news unless you got it from an official source. Even then be skeptical. Be careful about naming numbers of victims. It's much better to fill in the specifics later after the dust settles. It's generally okay to report what witnesses personally saw, but you have to be really sure of their credibility so you don't inflame a situation.

"Someone who lives in the apartment told me they'd been smelling a strong odor of natural gas all day, but we can't confirm yet if a gas leak led to this explosion."

"I talked with someone who was in the store when the shooting started, and she said she heard several rapid gunshots before she made it to the exit."

If that woman told me she saw six people dead, I'd be very skeptical about reporting that. How did she know they were dead? Six is a very specific number.

So much comes with experience and your judgment. Just remember that witnesses are emotional, excited, scared, and can be wrong much of the time. Don't report specifics about numbers, names, causes, or motives unless you've seen it yourself or you have confirmation from an official source. That includes what you post on social media! What you post has your name on it and is just as important and comes with the same responsibility as what you say on a broadcast.

Speaking of social media, you'll also want to make sure you post about your breaking story on your platform of choice. Include pictures and video if you can. Make sure when talking with witnesses that you ask them for video or pictures as well. Ask them if they can upload the files to your station's website or email them to you and make sure you get their written permission to use the materials per your company's policies.

When you're at breaking news, keep an eye out for surveillance cameras outside of businesses, or doorbell cameras on homes that might have caught some of the action. Knock on doors if you have time and ask if they can check their security video.

The best way to fill time and get out crucial information during breaking news is by interviewing someone live. You and/or your desk should make sure to put in requests with fire or police officials to see if they can get you a spokesperson to appear live on camera to help alert viewers about what's going on.

When you get that person on camera, be calm and ask them to go through the situation from the beginning to where things stand currently. They may not be able to tell you much, but just having them there to give you some facts is better than nothing.

Another important tip: When interviewing someone live, assuming you have a photographer working with you, make sure to position the person about to be interviewed to the side of you and back about two paces. Then, after you introduce the person, you need to pivot 180 degrees so your entire back is to the camera. The photographer can then zoom in to capture your interview subject with a nice full-frontal shot. If you stand side by side with your interview subject, the audience will see two bad profile shots as you turn inward to talk with each other. Sometimes it can't be helped, but it's much better if you can do "the pivot."

Filling time is extremely important during breaking news, especially if the video is captivating. You will earn huge points if you can keep the live shot going without having to rely on the anchors to help. But how do you know what else to talk about? We've mentioned describing your surroundings—what you can see, conditions, etc.—but there is also something you can do right now to help prepare for those breaking news situations that will help you your entire career.

Make an appointment to go talk to some firefighters at a local fire house. Tell them you're new in town, you're a reporter for a local station, and you want to learn about their job so you don't sound like an idiot when you're reporting on fires. Tell them you won't even bring a camera and you just want to learn. Sometimes, you might have to schedule this through a fire department Public Information Officer (PIO), but generally, they should be thrilled that you want to learn about their work.

Once you get to meet them, maybe bring some cookies as a thank you for their time. Ask them everything you want to know about fighting fires. What does a one-alarm, two-alarm, or three-alarm fire mean? How many fire stations are in the city? Why the different fire trucks or engines? What do they do? What does it mean when a fire is blazing and the smoke suddenly changes from black to white? Why do firefighters always have to get on the roof to fight house fires?

These are all facts you can use just about any time you report on fires, whether you're a reporter or maybe an anchor someday. Also make sure to hand out business cards at the end of the day, and tell them to call you if they ever have a story idea. This may have taken you all of two hours, but now you are so much more knowledgeable. And do the same thing with police. Ask them about crime scenes. How will you know if it's really serious? Can you go on a ride-along? Talk to the local district attorney. Have coffee with defense attorneys or judges. I'm sure you're getting the hang of it. This homework will really prepare you for breaking news, and it's something very few reporters will ever bother to do. I guarantee you if you're not shy and handle rejection well, you'll probably find plenty of professionals who'll be happy to teach you about their jobs, *and* they will be great resources later when you have questions about stories.

Finally, let's talk about your performance during breaking news. You want to be intense but calm. It's fine to refer to your notes. I really prefer notepads to cell phones for reasons we'll go into in the live shots chapter. Be confident. Tell viewers what you see and what you know. Don't guess. Don't relay information you have doubts about. If you're working alone, don't be afraid to tell viewers what you're doing so they can be included.

> *"Okay, I'm going to step over to the camera now so I can zoom in and show you what it looks like down this road where you can see police tape right there."*

It's fine. It's breaking news. It doesn't have to be super smooth. That's part of what makes it exciting. When you're reporting, once you've set the scene, start at the beginning,

> *"This came in as a call about a person having medical problems outside this store, but when police arrived the situation changed quickly."*

If the anchors ask you questions about something and you don't know the answer, say you don't know but will work to find out and get back to them. Don't BS or make anything up.

Breaking news is what some reporters live to cover. Others hate it. I always liked it. Sometimes it messed up the story I was previously working on, but I didn't mind. Some stories can be finished later. Just know that breaking news is a great opportunity for you to shine at your station. Do your homework beforehand. Don't speed. Be safe, and just tell us what you see. Back to you!

THE INTERVIEW

THIS CHAPTER HAS A LOT OF GROUND TO COVER, so I'm going to break it down into subheadings to make it easier to digest. Relax. Interviewing people is one of the most important parts of the job, and it's also fun. Some people are naturally curious, extroverted, and have a comfortable quality about them that makes it easy for others to talk with them. Some of us have to work harder at it and push ourselves to get quality sound. Either way, by the end of this chapter, you'll be much more prepared to get interviews and know what to do once you start whipping out the microphone.

Interviews are crucial opportunities for you to learn. Seek out different viewpoints, cultures, and perspectives for your story. And never worry about asking stupid questions; there are none.

If you need someone to dumb it down for you to understand, then assume the audience needs that help too. Be confident and ask anything you think is important.

SO MANY QUESTIONS

Every story you'll ever do will require you to ask questions. Really those are the first, second, and probably third steps you'll complete on any story. And that's before you even get to your interview. You might begin by asking questions of your coworkers.

> *"Hey, did you ever do a story on the snow up at Mount Hood? Where did you park? Is there a good lunch place on the way? Which ski shops will likely talk to me about their business?"*

Sometimes, you'll ask questions of people who will point you to other people who you'll question.

> *"Hey, Officer Johnston. Remember I talked with you last week out at that speed enforcement operation? Do you know of anyone we could speak with about stolen cars?"*

And almost every time, you'll ask questions of yourself.

> *"What else do I need to complete my story?"*

> *"Am I being fair?" "Who else can I talk to?"*

> *"Do I need graphics?"*

Finally, you will need to ask questions of the people who appear in your story—the interview. And while it may sound simple, it is more than just asking questions. In this chapter I will take you through the process of figuring out what questions to ask, how you should ask those questions, and what you should do with the answers. Let's begin with what can be the hardest part: How do you find an interviewee, and how do you convince that person to talk to you?

FINDING THE PERFECT INTERVIEW

So what do you want in an interview? Let's remember this is television. So you most want to interview someone who is engaging, speaks candidly, is knowledgeable about the subject, and most of all, someone who is available. That is the goal but not always the reality of what you'll be able to find in four hours. (Remember how long you have until you need to start writing and editing?)

I always liked doing television and never wanted to write for a newspaper, mostly because television is much more connected to the senses. Television does a really good job of conveying emotion. Now, I have teared up reading a newspaper story, but television has a great advantage over print or the written word. Print is really good for facts and figures. It can tell you exactly how much that bridge construction costs, how much it's over budget to the penny, and the exact dates each lane will be closed for the rest of the year. With print, if you don't understand all the information the first time you read it, you can go back as many times as it takes.

Television, or videos in general, aren't as good at conveying specific, complicated information. Let me say this again. Television is not well-suited for conveying complicated information, facts, and figures. That's why investigative pieces are so time-consuming and graphic intensive. Television is much better at conveying emotion, perspective, and the feeling of being there in the moment. So for our bridge example, you'd be wiser trying to explain the frustration of the commuter and the exasperation of the construction company because their supplier can't get them the materials on time. Television can show the crawl of cars and the backup into downtown causing problems for the pizza vendor because customers can't get to her shop.

TELEVISION EXCELS AT CAPTURING EMOTION. So we should strive to capture emotion in our interviews. Save only the most important facts and figures for your track. Generally speaking, don't ever let a spokesperson rattle off detailed facts and figures in your story. You can do that better with graphics (while making sure you only include what viewers really need to know). Instead, devote most of your story to the emotion and feelings you get from your interviews that can't easily be captured on paper. They have to be seen and heard to be fully appreciated.

TYPES OF INTERVIEWS

When you do interviews for a story, you'll basically interview "real" people and officials. "Real" people are neighbors, workers, voters, customers, business owners, gardeners, chefs, janitors, clerks, athletes, students, teachers, parents, victims, suspects, children, patients, nurses, some doctors. They are all people affected by the story and are not being paid in some capacity to speak to you. Most times, they are honest, candid, and will be able to tell you directly how the story has touched their lives.

The officials you'll interview include politicians, authors, spokes-people, police chiefs, medical or historical experts, corporate flacks, company executives, human resource officers, lawyers, and district attorneys. They are people who generally are being paid to talk to you or are using you in some way to get across information they want seen and heard. Therefore, they will have a definite slant or agenda in what they will say. They are pushing a certain point of view, which may or may not be the truth. It's almost certainly not objective. They will generally not be as can-did about your story.

I always prefer talking to "real" people. You may have to talk to a company official to get their side of the story. That's fine and expected, but don't ever stop there. The interesting interview for television is always the one with "real" people as they are more relatable to our audience. They use the same words and speak the same language as our viewers. Viewers can identify with "real" people because they may be or at least could be their neighbor. *If it could happen to them, it could happen to me,* they might think. So try to always include "real" people in every story you do.

Beyond all that, there is a third type of person. This is the person who you'll encounter most of the time. They are those who don't want to talk to you. They're afraid of cameras, or they're afraid of the subject matter. Maybe they're afraid someone will see them on TV and harass them. Maybe the subject matter is too sen-sitive. Maybe they just don't want to get involved. Sometimes they are worried the questions you ask and the answers they give might get them into trouble. Many, many times they don't want to be interviewed simply because they feel awkward and believe they'll look silly.

No matter who you're talking to, it's your job to convince them to go on camera! And it's also your job to listen to their concerns and realize they may have a legitimate reason for not wanting to talk to you. Maybe they are hiding from an abusive spouse. Maybe they're in a witness protection program. And when you consider that, it's probably an interview you can live without. It's okay to take no for answer. You're not a failure if you can't always get every interview. But you do need to work on your persuasion skills and ability to portray yourself as trustworthy to sources. **In almost all cases, you need to convince your subject that the opinion or information they have is important and worth sharing!**

LISTEN CAREFULLY

Now I want to talk about the importance of interviews, not just because they help fill out your stories and fill time, but because these people that you talk to one-on-one can really help you *understand* the story as a reporter. The experts and others you interview can clear up any confusion in your mind and help you focus on the most important point (you might never know unless you ask your own questions and then listen carefully to the answers). Interviews will point you in the direction of where the story is and where it can go.

Listening is a key part of the interview process. I've seen many reporters not really listening to the answers of the questions they just asked because they're busy staring at their notes trying to figure out what to ask next. Don't be locked in on what comes next. Concentrate on the present. Sometimes the best questions are asked based off the answers to the questions you just asked.

Imagine being sent to cover a story on an overnight break-in at a restaurant, and the place is a mess and the crooks stole the cash register. You go down there and find the owner sweeping up, and he agrees to speak with you. During the interview, after asking about what happened—how did they get in, what did they take—you take the next step and ask, "What does this loss mean to you as a small business owner?"

And the owner says, "Well, the loss of income hurts because my wife and I are taking care of our daughter at home who has been going through cancer treatment and can't get out of bed. This is going to be more money that we're now in debt." Such an answer could now set your story in a completely new direction. This new information has just made the story of a burglarized restaurant into the story of a man already in a desperate situation just hit with even more bad news. At the very least, I'd ask him if he would share a picture of his daughter or perhaps even be willing to let us come to his home and talk to his family. That's where the real story is, after all. If he agrees, you might not even want to start your story with video of the broken glass but instead start at the home to highlight that the victims aren't just businesspeople, but a family that was hurting and is now hurting even more.

Just one answer to a question can unlock everything for you. That's why it's so important to ask the basic questions and then ask what it all means (and make sure to listen to all the answers).

Many times I've interviewed victims of disasters. There are many who will not want to talk with you, which is understandable. They are traumatized and worried about bigger things than talking to a reporter. But you still have to ask. Because almost every time you'll find someone who wants to talk. I've always felt the people who consented to being interviewed by me after tragic situations felt a sense of relief to share their stories. In return, I always tried to be comforting, caring, and thoughtful about the questions I asked.

I've always felt when you're interviewing someone after a tragedy it's important to ask your questions in order of events because it's easier for them to remember and easier for you to tell their story. Here's an example of an interview you could conduct after a house fire:

> *"Okay. Tell me where you were in the house, what you were doing, and the first sign you noticed something was wrong."*

> *"I was in the bedroom sleeping and I smelled smoke."*

> *"Was there a fire alarm at all?"*

> *"No."*

> *"What happened next?"*

> *"I woke up my husband, and we turned on the light and noticed smoke coming in the vents."*

"What did you say when you saw that?"

"I said, 'My god, something's on fire! We gotta get out of here!'"

"What did you do next?"

"We grabbed our robes and bolted out of our bedroom, then ran down the hall and grabbed our kids and ran out the front door."

"Did your children know what was happening?"

"No, they were asleep. In fact, not even the fire engines woke them up."

"When you got outside what did you see?"

"The whole apartment next to us was on fire, and the fire engines were just getting to the complex."

"Did you see anyone in the apartment next door get out?"

"Yes, he got out. I saw the man who lives there along with his pet parrot on the lawn."

"Parrot?"

"Yes. He loves birds and has a big pet parrot named Charlie. All the kids play with him."

[Mental Note: I've got to find that parrot after I finish this interview.]

"So is there much damage to your apartment? What will you do next?"

"There is some smoke damage, but I don't think we lost anything."

"So this was a fire that woke you up in the middle of the night, but you got out safely with your kids. What is going through your mind now?"

"That it could have been a lot worse. We have our kids. We have each other. All that stuff in there doesn't mean anything. We are blessed that we got out and are safe."

That's an example of how I've conducted an interview many, many times. I covered the basics, I found an interesting tidbit, and I got the interviewee to put it all in perspective for me. I could go on the air and tell viewers about the fire, and if I could get the parrot, it'd be even better!

How many sound bites did you count in that interview? It was more than needed. And the way the questions were asked gives the story a beginning, middle, and end.

I'm sure you thought of some questions you might have asked. Was anything left out? Maybe ask if she knew what caused the fire; she might have known. Maybe she would have said she'd heard kids playing with fireworks behind the apartment last night. That information is not necessarily reportable, but it might be good background information to ask the firefighters about later.

All reporters have their own approach. You just want to make sure you don't miss the big things.

LOCATION, LOCATION, LOCATION

Where you interview your subject can be almost as important as who you interview. I always liked to get my interviews outside at the scene of the story. If you're doing a story about a bridge that is being renovated and need to talk to the construction manager, ask that person to meet you where there's a view of the bridge in the background. If the construction is causing a back-up for commuters trying to get to work, interview a commuter who is trying to get over the bridge in their car. So always try to interview your person in a setting that matches, but is not distracting from, the subject of the story. Please don't rely on web interviews unless absolutely necessary. If they can meet you at the location of your story, that also saves you precious time going to their office or their home. Let's face it, interviews behind a desk are visually boring. Avoid them. Convince the person you're interviewing that it will be more interesting, and comfortable, to talk outside where they can show you something. It's the truth, and if you present it that way, they will be more likely to agree. Also interviewing someone in a place of action gives you many options for shooting video of them in their element.

Sometimes, having an official meet you out at the story nucleus can give you a pass to get even closer to the action because you're with the boss. A construction foreman will be much more likely to let you get up close if the project supervisor has you in tow. So remember when making arrangements for that interview ask, "Hey can we meet you out at the scene?" More times than not, they'll be happy to, especially when you've explained the advantages for both of you.

CONFRONTATIONAL INTERVIEWS

People who work for large corporations will be very hard to get on camera. They are afraid of being fired. You might have luck at small, privately-owned companies, but there are no guarantees. Just because your odds aren't good, you still need to be able to say you tried to contact them, but they refused to comment.

Occasionally, you'll have to do interviews with people who hold very controversial views that will offend you. And in those cases, it will be very tempting for you to challenge the person you're interviewing about their opinions. And that's great! You should. But please remember to get what they really think on video first. Example: If you're interviewing a mayor who thinks that all city workers should be forced to read the bible on their breaks, your first question shouldn't be, doesn't this violate freedom of religion? You want what the mayor really believes on the record. So ask questions accordingly.

"Mayor Smith, you've been getting noticed lately because of your proposal about city workers. Tell me about it. Why do you want to do that? Do you think you can get it passed? How'd you come up with the idea?"

Then, once you have Mayor Smith's views recorded, you can start to ask questions that challenge that viewpoint and mention what critics are saying. If you start to provoke a subject too early, you run the risk of them tearing off the microphone and not talking to you. And while that may make for good theater, it's not good for your job of getting information out there. This goes for anyone who you feel may get angry or embarrassed and stop the interview at any moment. Get your interviewee's views on the record first, then ask the most difficult questions at the end. At the very least, you've recorded their views if they decide to terminate the interview.

THE VALUE OF THE MOS

When I was a young buck coming up through the ranks of TV news, I learned all about the time-tested interview all reporters have to someday come to terms with: the man on the street (MOS) interview. The goal of the MOS is to get the opinion of the average person out there. But it's easier said than done. I believe it's getting harder to get random strangers to talk to you. When I first started back in Fresno, people couldn't wait to be interviewed. They saw the camera and stood in line to give me their opinions about anything and everything. Now getting an MOS can be one the most challenging interviews a reporter does. People are more wary, especially of the media. They're afraid their opinions will be misconstrued or that they'll be targeted online if they have an unpopular opinion.

But MOS interviews are important for the truthfulness and candidness that we should always be searching for. If the local arena decides to raise concession rates, the team's owner is going to tell you all about the upgrades in food and service that justify the increase. But it's the average sports fan in line out front who will tell you how they simply can't afford to pay 15 dollars for a beer. And both sides are important to your story.

Sometimes getting strangers to talk to you on the street isn't so difficult. If the issue really gets people riled up, or if there are several people onsite, then you shouldn't have much trouble. That concessions example is a perfect opportunity for MOS interviews. But what about abortion? Good luck. What about new federal regulations on tires? Not likely. The issue has to be pretty well known and not too controversial for MOS interviews to be effective. Or the topic has to be something that hits really close to home for the interviewees.

We once had to cover a drowning at a lake. By the time we got there, the rescue teams were gone and there was no sign of the tragedy, just families out enjoying the water. If this were your story of the day, and knowing the rescue crews were gone, what would you do? Well, you've got to at least try to talk to people at the lake. And when you go to ask questions, you don't want to open with, "Hey, did you hear about the drowning out here today?"

A more effective approach would be, "Hey, how's it going? Nice day. I notice you have life jackets on your children, can we ask you a couple of questions about water safety?"

If they agree, you could then ask, "First, tell us why you like coming out here?" If they talk about how nice the lake is, you can use the clip in your story to reinforce how popular the lake is. Then you can ask why they put life jackets on their kids, and how they learned about that. Use those answers when you talk about the dangers of the lake or how many drownings they've had so far this year. Then *after* you've established rapport with them, you can ask them if they heard about the drowning. They might say yes, or that they just saw some rescue boats but didn't know what was going on. They might say they feel bad for that person's family. All are bites you can use for your story.

Most times, especially for delicate stories, you need to establish a conversation with the person before you point a camera in their face. You need to generally explain what the story is about, and then ask if it's okay to do an interview. And if they say something to you and later ask you to not use it, respect their wishes. This doesn't go for officials, but I think you should give "real" people some slack. Be outgoing and upbeat. Engage them. But also be respectful.

I think it's a great idea for you as a reporter/MMJ to have a go-to place for MOS interviews. Here are the ingredients which will give you the best chance at getting lots of good interviews: You need to find a location that has a steady stream of people coming so you have multiple chances to find someone who'll speak to you. It can't be in a mall or private parking lot because the owners can kick you out. And keep diversity in mind. You'll want your interview subjects to match the makeup of the community and you want people from all backgrounds. For me, the best places to get MOS interviews was an old-fashioned main street or a city park.

One of our reporters once set up in the town square with a posterboard on a stand that described the topic and gave instructions to step up to the microphone (set up on a light stand) to give an opinion, and it worked really well. The reporter and photographer could just sit down and relax and be super nonthreatening until someone strolling by said, "Yeah, I'd like to give my opinion on that." Genius. I wish I'd have thought of that.

Beyond getting the views of "real" people into your newscasts, MOS interviews can also be your last opportunity if you absolutely can't find any other kinds of interviews. You can almost always rely on the MOS to give some kind of opinion, and I always used to love an MOS to break up my reporter track and help tell the story. An MOS can provide reaction shots and opinions that will mirror some of your viewers'. In a way, an MOS is a representative of your audience that you include in real time in the story and a clever way to get that information out there.

THE WORST INTERVIEWS YOU'LL EVER HAVE

There will eventually come a time when you're asked to try to get an interview that will make you question whether you're in the right career, such as trying to get an interview with someone who has just lost a loved one, someone who was a victim of a crime, or someone who just lost their child. I don't think these interviews are easy for any of us, and at times we may question whether it's ethical or moral to bother someone when they are grieving or angry. News isn't math. There is not always a correct answer. But for what it's worth, I truly believe that it's our job to give these people an opportunity to speak about their loved ones or their situation.

To attempt to conduct these most difficult interviews, a phone call, a business card left on a doorstep, or a voicemail offering a platform to share are all possible ways in. If the individuals don't want to share, that's understandable. But as a journalist, you should not just assume they don't want to talk and therefore not try. Many people have agreed to talk about their loved ones with me, so I know better. Sometimes a spouse wants the community to know that their deceased wife was more than just a pedestrian. She was a nurse who cared for her patients, just got back from a bucket-list trip to Paris, and had a family that loved her. And the person who hit and killed her needs to be found.

But it's still not easy to make that initial call or knock on the door. It's the worst part of the job. I remember getting that dreaded assignment when a transportation employee was killed in a freak accident on a freeway. Our assignment desk found out where he lived, and they asked us to "swing by his house" to see if anyone had any reaction. We did head over there, and I was shocked to find a small but somber party going on in the backyard of his home with his adult children lighting candles and holding pictures. I approached without a photographer and told them who I was and if they would consider sharing a few words about their dad. They invited me in, hugged me, fed me food, and I spent the next hour there as they told me all about his life and his dream come true of living in America.

I'll never forget that day. They don't all turn out that way, but you just never know. Had I assumed they didn't want to talk, I'd have never met his family, and our viewers would have never known about the rich life he'd lived. You'll have to use your best judgment in these situations. In the end, the station won't know if you reached out or not. Just know that sometimes the door will be answered, and the story you will tell as a result will add depth, empathy, and perspective to what would have been just another statistic.

STAY CLOSE TO YOUR PHOTOGRAPHER

If you are lucky enough to be sent with a photographer, make sure to stick close to that person, not only for safety but also because you'll learn a lot. You'll see what kind of shots the photographer is getting, and that will help you later as you write. Don't be in your car on your phone while your photographer is working hard outside. Be invested and interested in the job they are doing. It will pay off.

The camera is like a beacon that says, "I'm from the TV news," and it attracts curious people. "Hey, are you guys from the news? What are you doing here?" Be patient and explain where you're from and what the story is about. I've gotten so lucky so many times in my career with people who wandered over and asked what we were doing and then either saw something or had information about the story we were covering. It's a great opportunity to meet people and gather information because they are *seeking you out.*

Also, if you are doing a large press conference with your photographer, make sure you stand close to them when you're asking questions of the person at the podium. That way when they answer your question, that person will be looking almost directly into your camera.

INTERVIEW TECHNIQUES

1. **ASK QUESTIONS KNOWING THERE ARE NO STUPID QUESTIONS.** Sometimes, you'll ask a question when you know the answer. But getting the answer and the emotion associated with that answer on video is what you're after. Asking a coach, "Hey, do you think you can beat the Broncos on Sunday?" may elicit a shake of the head from the coach, but you also may get a really good bite. "Of course we can win! That's why we're here! We've worked hard all week, and despite what the media seems to think about our chances, I think we can win, sure!"

2. **ESTABLISH A RAPPORT WITH THE PERSON YOU'RE INTERVIEWING BEFORE YOU PUT THE CAMERA ON THE TRIPOD.** Make small talk. Get to know the person. Reassure them you'll be respectful. You can tell them roughly what you're going to ask or what the subject matter is. Put them at ease and try to get them to lower their defenses.

3. **NEVER SUBMIT A LIST OF QUESTIONS AHEAD OF TIME TO SOMEONE YOU WANT TO INTERVIEW.** It's perfectly fine to say, I want to talk with you about _____, but do not give them your specific questions.

4.   **BE CAREFUL ABOUT PROMISING ANONYMITY TO YOUR INTERVIEWEE.** An interview in silhouette or not naming the source is done for safety reasons. Maybe they witnessed a gang shooting; maybe they are a whistleblower and fear retaliation from their boss. If you suggest anonymity, you need prior approval from your news manager so you're all on the same page. And if you include an interview with an anonymous source, don't put their name or picture anywhere on the raw video because later someone may come across your video, not knowing the situation, and boom, the source's name and picture get put on TV.

5.   **HAVE THE PERSON YOU'RE INTERVIEWING START AT THE BEGINNING AND TELL YOU THEIR STORY.** It's easier for them and will be easier for you later to make sense of it all.

6.   **TRUST YOUR GUT.** If you have doubts that your interview subject is telling the truth, don't use it.

TECHNICAL NOTES

- **FRAMING:** Always try to make sure when framing your interviewee that you can see both of their eyes so you don't get a profile shot.

- **STARTING:** ALWAYS, ALWAYS, ALWAYS, start every interview (once you're rolling video) by asking them to say their name and title and then have them spell it. This is crucial so you can make sure to have that important information when writing your story. Also, it's very helpful for anyone back at the station. If they want to use your raw video for another story, they will know who is on the video.

Having them **pronounce** their own name also prevents embarrassing mistakes later.

- **TWO-SHOTS**: If you have a photographer working with you and want to do a walking interview, it's best to keep it a wide two-shot so both you and the interview subject are in the frame. Having the photographer zoom in on your interviewee while walking accentuates the up and down movement and it can look jarring on the screen. Keep it a two-shot the entire time.

- **MICROPHONES**: Oh boy. I'm opening up a can of worms here, I know. Generally, for indoor interviews, one-on-one interviews with a main subject of your story in quieter environments, or walking interviews, I prefer lavaliere microphones. But for MOS, and especially breaking news situations, I much prefer hand or stick microphones. Stick mics with or without station logos are great for interviewing multiple people one after the other without giving them the chance to change their minds as you attach the lav (lavalier) mic. Stick mics are also great for interviews or stand-ups when there is loud background noise. Make sure in those loud environments you hold the microphone very close to the mouth (within three inches). Some photographers will argue against using the stick microphone because they feel it makes the aesthetics of the shot look bad. But I believe there is a place for it. In breaking news situations when it's noisy, or you may have to interview someone at a moment's notice. Also, for pushing your station brand and logo, I believe the stick or hand microphone is the optimal choice.

FINAL THOUGHTS ON INTERVIEWS

The best policy you can have as a reporter is to make every effort to get out of the station, get to the scene, and try. You never know what you'll find. If ten people say no and one says yes, that's success.

Just know there will always be people who won't talk to you no matter what. Be smart about where you look for interviews. Always be safe, be honest with those you speak with, and let them point the way to your true focus.

B-ROLL

I CALLED MY LONG-TIME FRIEND Oscar Deleon this morning to get his take on the subject of B-roll. He was one of my favorite photographers back in the day when I was a brand-new reporter working my first TV job in Fresno. B-roll is a term we TV people use to this day, and I thought I knew where it came from, but I wanted to get more specifics from Oscar. He started working as a photographer in the 1970s when news was shot on film.

Oscar told me that he would go out with or without a reporter and shoot the news of the day on 16-millimeter film. Then, after the story was shot, he'd go back to the station, develop the film, then literally slice and glue the film together to make the story (editing). So as an editor you'd cut one piece of film with all the sound, another piece of film with all the pictures, and they'd go on different projectors. Back then you needed chemicals, fancy equipment, and time! Now we can do it on our phones. Crazy, right?

When doing a story that included shots of the location and a soundbite, it was difficult to time out how long the anchor would speak before you needed to hear and see the soundbite. So TV stations back then created a system where one projector would have the A-roll, which is any film that had sound up full, such as a soundbite or interview. The other projector would hold the B-roll, all the film showing the location or other story images. The director would dissolve between the two depending on whether the script called for images or sound. How they ever managed all that I can't even imagine.

Fast-forward to when videotape started replacing film in the late 1970s and early 1980s. The term B-roll stayed and does to this day. Once in a while, you'll hear someone say, "We need to get some A-roll," as in interviews, but it's pretty seldom. So now that you know where the term B-roll comes from, let's talk about what you want to look for to get all the pictures for your story that do not include traditional interview sound.

I want to make clear, I'm not a photographer. I never had to shoot my own video. But I was on the hip of many photographers in my day, and I had to do a lot of editing in my career, so I know what makes up good video even if I haven't physically shot it myself.

The first thing you need to do is figure out the focus of the story, and then make sure you get those shots. If you're doing a story at a high school football game about a prom queen who doesn't know her father is coming back from the army overseas, she hasn't seen him in two years, and he's going to take off the school mascot costume to surprise her, you'd want a few shots of the game, the crowd, and the players. But mostly, you'd want to focus on the girl and the mascot before the big moment. And you'd want to make sure you were in the right position and recording when the mask came off. You'd also want some shots of the two main subjects before it all happened so you could build excitement in your story.

Some stories you cover won't be so specific, or you won't know the focus until you really start to dive into it. I've been on many stories where I didn't find the focus until I was almost done with all the interviews and shooting video. But the sooner you can find the focus, the more you can concentrate on the shots you'll really need to tell the story. Until you find the angle you're going to take, you'll have to get a little bit of video of everything, which isn't ideal.

In all cases, no matter what you shoot, here are my seven B-roll must-dos:

1. **A SCENE SETTER:** This is a wide shot of the story location— the outside or inside of a stadium, the front of an office building, the sign that has the town's name at the city limits line. It's a great shot to start any story. You don't always have to use it, but you'll be glad you got it. You'll also want to get an introductory shot if you're doing a story about one or two people. It's a shot of

them walking, working, doing.

2. **WIDE SHOTS:** These shots show the scale of your story—maybe a wide shot of a theater showing the stage and crowd and orchestra. If a guy is fishing on the side of the lake, you want a shot that shows how big the lake is compared to the guy. Wide shots are important because they give the viewer perspective. How big is the area we're talking about? I'd want to see everything in one shot.

3. **MEDIUM SHOTS:** These are the most common waist-high or eye-level shots of people that mimic what the eye sees as you walk around. They are important, may fill the bulk of the video you'll use, and are easy to see and understand as a viewer. They usually aren't jarring, and give viewers a good sense of what's going on. They're also the easiest to get as a photographer because they don't require a lot of effort or thought. But don't rely on medium shots. You're better than that. Medium shots are the vanilla ice cream in a banana split. They are useful but don't really give us the rich perspective of the wide or, my favorite, tight shots. You need to get the chocolate sauce, whipped cream, and nuts for your story!

4. **TIGHT OR CLOSE-UP SHOTS:** As a reporter/MMJ these should be your favorite shots to get because they give you texture, fine details to write about, and they are the heart of the story. Close-ups of the hands of a third grader shaking hands with an elderly volunteer, the wrinkles around the eyes, the blinking light in the control panel of a factory, a few blades of grass

getting stomped by a football cleat—close-ups are where it's at. Make sure you look around and notice the fine details of your story and get at least five good close-ups. You will be so happy you did later when you're looking through your video and figuring out what to write.

5. **SEQUENCING:** Photographers love shooting in locations where the same thing happens over and over again, such as on a factory floor. This is your opportunity to get three shots that you can later edit together to really put the viewer there. A wide shot of the whole factory, a medium shot of the woman at the sewing machine, and a tight shot of her fingers sewing the white laces onto a football. Look to build sequencing any time you see repetitive actions in a story you're doing. You won't get this every story, so when the opportunity presents itself, do it.

6. **CONTRASTS AND SIMILARITIES:** As a photographer, always be on the lookout for contrasts and similarities. Those visuals help give you moments to write about and new areas to investigate. Maybe you're doing a story on a new park or school that's opening. Maybe you not only want to show the new and shiny but also go to an area that has the oldest park or the oldest school. How is life for them? Contrasting elements offer great opportunities. Busy, slow; big, little; city, country; urban, forest. Look for what's common and for what's different. Highlighting those adds more texture to your story and gives you new angles to explore.

7. **NATURAL SOUND:** This is what I think may be most important. Natural sound is noise that you find at the location of your story that you didn't elicit. So it's not an interview, but it could be an announcer on a loudspeaker, a band, the sound of a chainsaw or heavy machinery, or nature sounds like a waterfall or dog barking. The noises add dimension and depth to your story. They provide a way to break up your narration track and sound bites. They provide pacing and really help the viewer to experience what you saw and heard when you were there. If you allow your ears to guide your eyes when searching for shots when you're on a story, the sounds will usually take you to action. And everyone knows action shots are more exciting. When you first get to the location of your story, listen. **Go toward the noise and investigate.** If what you discover fits into your story then those are the sounds and pictures you will want to shoot, write to, and edit into your story.

A few other suggestions: Walking shots are great, and I highly advise getting a couple on every story you do. Take the camera, put it on your shoulder, and walk around to show viewers what it feels like being there. But for all other shots, please USE A TRIPOD. You want your non-walking shots to be rock steady and in focus. They are a sign of professionalism and will set you apart from the competition. It's hard to carry that tripod around, yes, but so worth it. And if you're a reporter working with a photographer, offer to carry the tripod. It's the least you can do.

Don't forget about getting video from down on the ground (literally place the camera on the ground) or from up above. High- and low-angle shots are great for showing different views and can really help out in the editing process.

Don't overuse camera movement by constantly, panning, zooming, or tilting the camera. Those shots should be used to show relation and context, sometimes for effect. But you don't want your story filled with moving camera shots, unless that's the look you're going for. Mostly use wide, medium, and close-ups that are steady. They should be your bread and butter.

Also when shooting, don't forget to let the camera roll to **shoot long shots**. Each shot should be at least seven to ten seconds long. There's going to be a little jiggle when you hit record and when you hit stop, so that's a second wasted on either end. Don't hit record for only three seconds and call it good. You will be very frustrated when you go to edit. Give yourself room and time. After you hit record, wait a couple of seconds before you start counting.

Shooting video is an art all its own, but it should always be done with a purpose and with the goal of communicating your story, not distracting from it. Look for shots for the opening of your story, and keep an eye out for shots that would be great for the last video of the piece. If you can identify those while you're out shooting your story, it will make your writing that much easier later in the day.

STAND-UPS

THE INFORMATION I'LL PRESENT IN THIS CHAPTER will be similar in some ways to the next chapter on live shots, but there are some important differences. Let's begin!

Stand-ups are the part of the package or story you create where you get to stand in front of the camera and tell or show the audience something. If you're a reporter or MMJ who doesn't appear on the news set very often or in live shots, the stand-up is valuable to show your face so viewers can form a better connection with you. And you want a strong connection with our audience.

Let me clarify the difference between a stand-up and a live shot. A stand-up is a ten- to fifteen-second piece of your story where you appear on camera within the story itself. The stand-up is not live. You record it and then insert it into the middle or end of your story while you're editing. A live shot, or even a taped version of a live shot, sometimes called a "look-live," involves you standing in front of the camera and introducing and then tagging your story. The anchor introduces you and your story and tosses to you live. Then you would tell the audience more about where you are and you would toss to your story. When the story ends, you would immediately appear again on camera live, and you would then wrap up the story and toss back to the anchors.

If you do a live shot you may not want to include the stand-up in your story because it might be too much of you. But if you're live in an earlier show, they might want to use your stand-up for the version of the story that airs later that night. That is NOT what this chapter is about. We'll cover live shots a little later in this book.

So as we turn our attention to stand-ups let's begin by talking about their purpose. In my time as a reporter, I've come up with the most frequent reasons to do a stand-up:

1. **DEMONSTRATION:** The best, easiest, and most effective use of a stand-up is to show or demonstrate something for the audience. Remember show-and-tell in kindergarten? That's the idea here. Show viewers how something works. Show what happens when you walk through the door of that haunted house. Reveal an object so viewers can see it in your hands because we're really experiencing this story through you (this is the best reason to do a stand-up, and you should

be looking for these opportunities). Move and walk if possible. Don't just stand there. If you're an MMJ, get creative, and try to do something so you won't end up being a lump in the middle of the frame.

2. **SHOWING PERSPECTIVE:** If you're doing a story on a huge new theater, a great way to show how big it is might be you standing on the stage and then zooming back to show us the entire auditorium. Viewers know how big a person is, and with you as a reference they get a great sense of size. Of course, this can be next to impossible for an MMJ. But still try to be creative. Anytime you can add perspective by using yourself as a model or size reference, that's a great reason for a stand-up.

3. **MOVEMENT IN TIME AND PLACE:** Stand-ups are great opportunities to lead the viewer by the hand and show them the way when your story takes an abrupt turn in either time or location. "As you can see, this area is totally clean now, but just twenty-four hours ago, this entire beach was a mess." Then show video of what it looked like the day before. The same goes for places. Moving from place to place or city to city can be confusing in a story, but stand-ups can make it clear. "This is where the car ended up on this street in Clovis over by that broken fence right there. But this chase actually began in the arrivals level at the airport." Boom. Viewers are right with you. They know where it ended and where you're going now. Explaining changes in locations and times are great uses of stand-ups.

4. **COVER VIDEO:** There are times when you need to say something in a story that is very important, but you

just don't have any video to use to cover your voice track. It's action or information that is vital to the story, and you know you'll have to include it, but you just don't have video. Or even if you shot that video, it would be boring to watch, such as shots of a building or other location. This is where a stand-up describing what happened can be valuable. It's never ideal, but in many cases, it's better than graphics or a map to explain this crucial detail. "The court papers say the officer came to this house behind me and was greeted by not one, but three pot-bellied pigs that lunged at him and knocked him right into this mailbox." That stand-up with your delivery is far better than seeing a shot of the house and panning to the mailbox. It's important when you're out shooting your story to realize when you're going to run into trouble editing your story and will need this kind of stand-up to bridge the gap between what you have to say but lack the video you need.

5. **REACTION:** This one is seldom done but can be most effective. I usually use it on feature stories when I'm reacting to something funny or interesting done by the person I'm featuring. It may be just a nod of the head, a laugh, or a look of surprise. But these little reaction stand-ups can be gold when you're editing your piece. The reason why they're effective is because they help put the audience in your place. The viewer may be just as shocked as you when the lady told you that you should try belly dancing with her. Your horrified reaction helps the viewer identify

with you. They can be great if done right, but use these shots sparingly.

I should explain what makes a bad stand-up and how many stand-ups you should do in a day, a week, or in one piece. I think the golden rule to a lot of things you'll do—editing, writing, performance, etc.—comes down to this: Is what you're doing adding to or taking away from the story? You may think of a great stand-up, but if the viewer is so awestruck by what you've done that they don't pay attention to the next few lines of the story, then maybe you've gone too far. Do not distract from the story! Live by that rule and you'll be okay. Just because you think of something doesn't mean you have to do it.

I think personally, you should try to do a stand-up in every story (package) you do unless you're going to toss to it live. Even then, you should probably shoot one in case another show wants to use it. As I said, it's a great way to build that connection with the viewer. A stand-up turns you from a voice to a face with eyes they can see. It's not about selfish "face time" or that you want to be famous. It's about building that connection with the audience. And stand-ups are one way to build that relationship.

That said, there were many times when I felt a stand-up in the story would be inappropriate. Usually, it was sensitive stories where I was talking with someone one on one. It felt to me, pulling away from that with a stand-up would have lessened the impact of what I was doing with the other part of the story.

Sometimes, I just couldn't think of a stand-up that would make sense. That's okay. Don't force it. Better no stand-up in a piece than one that's awkward. There are times when you might want to do more than one stand-up in a piece or a series of stand-ups to get your point across, but that is the rare exception. If you're doing two or three stand-ups in one piece, multiple times a month, I personally think that's too much. You need to get better at telling the story with video rather than viewers just seeing you.

Every station should have a policy on stand-ups, but few do. If I were the news director, I'd want to see you in every package unless you're live. Try to figure out what your station's policy is. And in time, you'll develop your own internal policy as to when to shoot one and when not to. If in doubt, always shoot one. You can always decide not to use it later.

One final, very important thought. As a young reporter, it was hard for me to think of what to say in a stand-up for a story I wasn't even sure how to write yet, and that can be a problem for a lot of folks. Just keep this in mind: **A stand-up is NOT a small, condensed version of your story**. It's not a summary. It's only a piece of your story. It doesn't have to be long; in fact, it's better if it's not. Three lines, about ten seconds is ideal. Show something!

> *"And this here is the smoke jumper's parachute. It weighs about ten pounds. Not the heaviest gear but without a doubt the most important."*

There's a stand-up for a story on smoke jumpers who para-chute into wild land fires. You don't know what the rest of the story will be about yet, but you know you can throw this stand-up in just about anywhere. I always got into trouble when I made my stand-up a mini version of my story. Then when it came to plugging it in, it wouldn't work because I'd already addressed part of what my stand-up said, and the rest was coming later in the story. **Remember: Stand-ups are just a piece of the puzzle.** If you demonstrate something you see or something visual, they are easier to do on the spot without even having to write anything.

After a while, you'll get good at spotting these opportunities. They are small details of the larger story that you can draw atten-tion to by talking about them on camera and showing viewers! Kindergarten, remember? Show-and-tell.

It's that easy...sort of.

WRITING

I'M BEING BRUTALLY HONEST IN THIS BOOK by telling you about the world of news, hoping you'll take what you need to be ahead of the game. This is the chapter I've both dreaded and couldn't wait to write because of all the skills I had as a reporter, I felt writing was what I did best. I could devote a whole book to writing and there would still be more I'd want to say. I don't want to overwhelm you, so I will try to keep this as short as I can while still giving you what you need to know to write stories as a television reporter. A lot of what I'm about to tell you goes hand in hand with my style and the way I write. You will develop your own style that may be very different from mine. That's great! But I'm also hoping you'll take some fundamentals from this chapter that you can use with any style. Are you ready? Pour yourself a cup of coffee because you may need it. Let's go.

Let's begin with the goal of what you're trying to accomplish when writing for TV: **Concisely and clearly communicate a story to the viewer that complements your pictures, natural sound, and interviews.** Your writing is the thread that weaves together the different elements into the fabric that conveys ideas that, hopefully, touch viewers. Another goal is also to tell a story that is easily understood and doesn't take sides—a story that presents facts and emotions, enlightens, is not boring, and sometimes is entertaining. The rest—having the right tone and dynamic, adding in a splash of creativity and a bit of poetry—will come with time and experience. It's not necessary to have all these aspects every day in every story. At first, just focus on telling a simple story.

The first mistake that nearly all inexperienced TV reporters/ MMJs make is trying to say too much. They figure they've gone and interviewed all these people, gathered all these facts, and shot all this video. It'd be such a waste not to include everything! The problem is, you're doing a 90-second story, not an hour-long documentary. I'm not great at math, but I do have a few "Wayne Formulas" that deal with TV reporting. One is the more you say, the longer your story will be, and the more confusing your story will be to viewers. That's why when you are sent to cover a story, quickly find your focus. You can't possibly tell everything there is to know about your story, so find the most important, most interesting part and say that. With TV news, the old adage "less is more" really does apply. So, rule number one in TV writing is **narrow your focus.**

There are many ways reporters write stories, but I'll share the way I found works best. Once I'd done all the interviews and my photographer had shot all the video, there wasn't anything I could do at that stage to change what we'd just done. Those puzzle pieces were set. The only changeable factor to make all the pieces fit together was my writing. If the interviews left something important out, I needed to make sure I wrote that in my reporter track (the words that you'll later narrate to form your voice track).

So if you have time, the first step is to log the video that you shot. Listen to and transcribe the interviews, noting the time-code of where these interviews and soundbites are. Timecodes are the internal clock that you find superimposed on raw video that helps you reference a specific point so an editor or writer or you can later find it. If you're in a rush, you only need to transcribe the parts of the interviews you think have a good chance of making it into your story.

Then you need to look at the B-roll and see if any particular scenes jump out at you. Sometimes I'd see B-roll that would make me think of a line I could write in my track. In your notes, write that line and timecode of the shot so you can find it later. Maybe you see a close-up shot of a whistle around a coach's neck, and he blows the heck out of it. You might want to talk about how the whistle is one of his tools and you could even do a montage of him blowing the whistle during different parts of the practice. Take note of these interesting shots to see if there's a way you can refer to them in your story.

Once I had identified the best soundbites from all the interviews, I would lay them out in the script in the order that made the most sense. I'd put in six or eight soundbites at this stage of my writing, but I probably only had room for four soundbites. If there's a stand-up, I'd put that into place in the script as well. If there was natural sound, I'd put that in usually at the beginning of the story and maybe again somewhere else.

So now you have all your interview and natural (nat) sound written into your draft of the script and you cannot change those elements. So now your job is to write a script that connects all these pieces of sound together and tells the story of what you're trying to communicate. It sounds complicated, but it's really pretty simple once you do it this way a few times. As you start writing, you can then narrow down which of the extra bites you can get rid of so that your story hits the total time your producers have allowed you. Sometimes you'll need to trim bites to the most important sentence to make it all fit.

In the following example, I picked a random topic to show you the rough draft, improved draft, and final draft of my story. Follow along to see what changes I made and why.

We first start by laying in all the sound we think we might want to use—the best, most concise, hopefully emotional bites from all your interviews. This story is about a strike at a school district where you spent the day on the picket line talking with workers, the district, and parents.

VERSION 1 (SOUND ONLY):

Nat sound chanting at 34:09: "We're not going back, without a contract!"

SOT 36:12: "I can't afford to live on what they're paying me. But it's not only money. Our health benefits suck. I had to wait three months before they'd approve surgery on my knee last year."

SOT 37:12: "We're being asked to do more with less! Right now I have thirty-seven students. Thirty-seven in one class! There's no way anyone could teach that many kids at one time. We need more teachers, more aides, and more help before it's too late."

SOT 39:13: "I feel bad for the kids missing school, but if we don't fight for them now, it's just going to get worse and worse for them. It's their education that's suffering, and that's why we need to take a stand now."

SOT 44:19: "We don't comment on pending negotiations. All we can say is we hope to get teachers back to school as soon as we can. We're meeting with teachers again tonight, and hopefully we'll make some headway by tomorrow. But even if we get an agreement tonight, we wouldn't be able to ramp up school by Monday."

Stand-up: 49:12: "The Ortega family has a front-porch view of this strike. That's their house right there across the street. And like thousands of families in this district, they want their children back in school now."

SOT 45:21: "I have to miss work to watch my two kids. I can't miss work much more, or they will fire me. And my kids just sit at home. It's not good. They need to settle this strike very soon."

SOT 45:51: "It's hard hearing those teachers chanting all day. I think the district should give them what they want. I support the teachers 100 percent."

Shot at 58:13: Sandwich shop bringing in food for teachers

Nat sound 43:10: Horns honking and fists raising from passing cars supporting teachers

So there is the first draft of the script. I have all the good bites and natural sound logged and in an order that makes sense to me. I can move it around later if I want. And I know I'm going to have to get rid of some of it. If you just added up the time of all these nat sounds and bites I'm already at 1:23 or so. That's without any of my track that I still have to write. The producers were nice to me and said I could have 1:45 for this story, but I will have to do some trimming before I can send in this story.

Now it's time to add in the words I will record for the voice track. My goal is to tell the story, connect these soundbites, and do it with the least writing possible to make sure my story hits its allotted total time.

VERSION 2 (WITH ROUGH TRACK):

Nat sound chanting at 34:09: "We're not going back without a contract!"

Track: About thirty teachers carried signs and chanted outside Burton Elementary School as day three of the Miller School District teachers' strike arrived with no end in sight.

SOT 36:12: "I can't afford to live on what they're paying me. But it's not only money. Our health benefits suck."

SOT 37:12: "We're being asked to do more with less! Right now I have thirty-seven students. Thirty-seven in one class! There's no way anyone could teach that many kids at one time."

Track: Teachers want a five percent raise and want the district to commit to hiring fifty more teachers in the next three years. Teachers say while the strike hurts now, the goal is to ultimately help students.

SOT 39:13: "I feel bad for the kids missing school, but if we don't fight for them now, it's just going to get worse and worse for them."

Track: The school district has said in the past they don't have the money to meet teachers' demands. Today, the superintendent wouldn't talk about specifics.

SOT 44:19: "We don't comment on pending negotiations. All we can say is we hope to get teachers back to school as soon as we can. We're meeting with teachers again tonight, and hopefully we'll make some headway by tomorrow."

Stand-up: 49:12: "The Ortega family has a front-porch view of this strike. That's their house right there across the street. And like thousands of families in this district, they want their children back in school now."

SOT 45:21: "I have to miss work to watch my two kids."

Track: Maria Ortega is worried about losing her job, as she now has to stay home to watch first-grader, Sally, and Ruben who is in third grade.

SOT 45:51: "I think the district should give them what they want. I support the teachers 100 percent."

Shot at 58:13: Sandwich shop bringing in food for teachers

Track: Besides Mrs. Ortega, the teachers also have the support of some local businesses as a local sandwich shop dropped off free subs and drinks.

Nat sound 43:10: Horns honking and fists raising from passing cars supporting teachers

Track: And there is also the constant stream of cars passing by, many honking and shouting their support.

The district says teacher reps will sit down with the district again tonight to try to settle the strike, but the superintendent says even if they reach an agreement, they won't be able to get kids back in class until sometime next week.

In Skyville, Wayne Garcia, News 10.

Okay. Version 2 has everything I want, but it times out to about two minutes. So we have to cut about fifteen more seconds. Let's have at it one more time!

VERSION 3 (FINAL VERSION):

Nat sound chanting at 34:09: "We're not going back without a contract!"

((SUPER; :00 Skyville))

Track: About thirty teachers carried signs and chanted outside Burton Elementary School on day three of the Miller District School strike.

SOT ((SUPER: Myron Baker/Teacher)) 36:12: "I can't afford to live on what they're paying me. But it's not only money. Our health benefits suck."

SOT ((SUPER: Molly Turner/Teacher)) 37:12: "We're being asked to do more with less! Right now I have thirty-seven students. Thirty-seven in one class! There's no way anyone could teach that many kids at one time."

Track: Teachers want a five percent raise and the district to commit to hiring fifty more teachers over the next three years. Teachers say while the strike hurts now, the goal is to help students.

SOT ((SUPER: Pete Peters/Teacher)) 39:13: "I feel bad for the kids missing school, but if we don't fight for them now, it's just going to get worse and worse for them."

Track: The school district has said in the past they don't have the money to meet teachers' demands. Today, the superintendent wouldn't talk about specifics.

SOT ((SUPER Dr. Clyde Jefferson/Superintendent)) 44:19: "We don't comment on pending negotiations. All we can say is we hope to get teachers back to school as soon as we can. We're meeting with teachers again tonight, and hopefully we'll make some headway by tomorrow."

Stand-up: ((SUPER: Wayne Garcia/News 10)) 49:12: "The Ortega family has a front-porch view of this strike. That's their house right there across the street. And like thousands of families in this district, they want their children back in school now."

SOT 45:21: "I have to miss work to watch my two kids."

Track: Maria Ortega says she could lose her job, as she now has to stay home to watch first-grader, Sally, and Ruben who is in third grade.

SOT ((SUPER Maria Ortega/Parent)) 45:51: "I think the district should give them what they want. I support the teachers 100 percent."

Shot at 58:13: Sandwich shop bringing in food for teachers

Track: Besides parents like Maria Ortega, the teachers also have the support of some local businesses. We saw this sandwich shop dropping off free subs and drinks.

Nat sound 43:10: Horns honking and fists raising from passing cars supporting teachers

Track: And you can also hear support from passing cars.

Even if both sides agree on a contract tonight, the superintendent says it will be next week before students can return to class, and that's the best-case scenario.

In Skyville, Wayne Garcia, News 10.

Now we're timing out right at 1:45. You can see the painful process of trying to trim soundbites without changing their meaning and cutting your own words down to fit all the important material into the time frame you've been given. In the last version, I also added in names and titles. I could cut this to 1:10 if I had to, but you'll find sometimes doing shorter stories takes you longer to write because there is just no room for any fat. Literally each word has to be perfect. If the story had to be shorter, we'd have to lose some soundbites. That's why reporters always fight to have longer stories. But they don't usually make the case for longer story times in the morning meeting. It's usually thirty minutes before airtime that you hear reporters begging producers for more time. At that point it forces the poor producer to cut something they've worked hard on to accommodate you. So just be aware that it's important to come very close to hitting your allotted time for your package. If it's really something you need more time for, reach out to managers or producers earlier in the day and make your case. Chances are, they'll say go for it.

SO HOW DO YOU WRITE?

Okay, Wayne, I get it so far, but how do YOU write? How do you know what to say, make sure you include the important information, and get it done on time?

Well, it's not always easy. There are a million ways to write a story. I believe the biggest factor that plays into the way I write a story is time. How much time do I have before the script has to be done, and how much time do I have to tell the story within the newscast? You can write the greatest story ever told, but if it doesn't make slot or appear on the newscast at the time it's expected, you're going to be in trouble. Two different time considerations dictate how I write the story:

1. how long I have to actually write the story, and
2. the length of the story itself.

Those factors can vary greatly. I've written a story in five minutes, and I've taken a week to write one. I've written packages as short as thirty-five seconds and as long as thirteen minutes. Advantages and limitations of different scenarios:

1. YOU HAVE A GREAT STORY AND THEY'VE GIVEN YOU AMPLE TIME TO BOTH TELL AND WRITE IT.

This can be the best of all circumstances for a reporter. You have great interviews and video, and you know this is going to be one very special story. So you've convinced the news director to give you the whole day to write it, and it won't air until tomorrow! Fantastic. And because the story has the potential to be so good, they've said you can have four minutes in the newscast.

To me this can be good and bad news. Good because I can relax a little and take my time, but now there is pressure to deliver on my promise that this will be a great story. If I had a really touching interview that turned out great, I put a lot of pressure on myself to make sure my writing lives up to the great potential of what could be.

If you have ample time, you want to make sure you log (transcribe) all the interviews, write down where all the great shots are, spend a good amount of time crafting the anchor intro, and then lay in all the best sound first (like the writing exercise in the prior section). Know that because your story is long, it's also going to take a long time to edit. Make sure to give your editor (or yourself) at least two to three hours to edit it together. The last thing you want to do is rush the editing after you've spent so much time getting the writing just the way you want it.

When you have time to write, you want to put in maximum effort for each word to be perfect. You want to think about your approach and come up with the perfect ending. In this scenario, you want to give the story everything you've got. You have the luxury of time to think, plot, and try different options until you hit on the one that really works. This should be an example of the very best that you can do. Savor the moment. There will be only a few days like this a year.

2. YOU HAVE A SHORT TIME TO WRITE AND A SHORT STORY TO TELL.

This is what you'll deal with most of the time. The story you're covering is pretty simple—one or two interviews, a basic issue to explain. The producer wants a 1:30 package, and you have an hour or less to write. These are the stories where you bang it out without worrying about finesse. Get it done. Be accurate. Tell the story. Be clear and get it edited and sent into the station. If you are short on time to write, you may not even log the bites from the interviews. You'll rely on your memory as to what was said, and you'll pick and insert the soundbites as you're editing then transcribe it later. Keep your tracks simple and short. Get it done.

3. YOU HAVE A COMPLICATED STORY, AND A SHORT TIME TO WRITE IT.

This is the doomsday scenario for any reporter or MMJ. You have a lot of material to cover, but for some reason you have less than an hour, maybe only thirty minutes to write. Maybe the governor you had to interview was late. Perhaps your key interview had much more interesting material than you thought, and also you had to spend a lot of time convincing her to speak to you. Maybe the location was changed at the last minute, and you had to drive to a different town to get the main part of your story. Whatever the reason, you are now under the gun, sweating bullets and super stressed because you know this story will be hard to write and the clock is ticking. In these cases, you need to quickly distinguish between what the plan was versus what actually can be done now. Then get started.

Maybe a producer can help you by doing a quick preview story that explains the issue and you can just do the reaction. If you're in multiple newscasts, maybe you can just do a couple of straight soundbites for the first newscast and then do a more in-depth story for later. Whatever your solution, you need to come up with it quickly and make it work because not being able to file your story on time is not an option.

Remember, keep it simple, focus not on the entire overarching issue but one part of it, the most interesting part. Don't try to say too much. This is hardest to remember when you don't have time to really filter out the unnecessary. But be realistic. If you think you can get it all finished in time, great. But if you have doubts, adjust as soon as you can.

Usually, this situation doesn't just sneak up on you unless there is some kind of equipment failure. So if you can see this kind of problem developing earlier in the day, do everything you can to prepare for it. Maybe send your first interview back to the station and have them work with that, and you'll do only the second part.

The last thing you want to do is plod ahead like everything is fine. At some point, you'll need to either cut down your story or find a different way to present it if you don't have enough time. Time is everything in our jobs. There's never enough of it.

Let's now move on to the more tangible, "how to" part of writing to make it the best it can be.

WHERE TO START

Unless you are really under the gun and have zero time, always strive to write your story in the order it will be seen by the viewer. That means writing the anchor intro first.

If you're doing a live shot, the next step is to write your live intro, then the package, then your tag, then the anchor tag (if there is one). There are a few reasons I do it this way and advise all reporters to do the same.

First, it just makes sense to write in this order. Before you can write your package you have to know where you are in the storytelling process. And it's important to remember that **each segment, anchor intro, reporter intro, package, and live-shot tag are all different elements.** All those pieces should work together in layers to reveal something new, set the stage, and finally tell the story. The anchor intro and your intro should never be mini versions of the story. Each has a different purpose and should include different details and information to move the story forward. Let's quickly break down those elements.

ANCHOR INTRO

This is what the anchors say when they introduce you or your story. This is one of the most important parts of your story because it will either raise viewer interest and cause them to turn up the volume so they can see this great story unfold or say, "Boring, meh, I'm not interested, let's see what Judge Judy's got."

Unfortunately, many reporters write the anchor intro last because they are rushed, worn out from getting their story to editing, or just want to get ready for the live shot and be done. "Yeah, let me put something for the anchors to read. They can always fix it if they don't like it."

Nope. No one knows your story better than you. Therefore, no one can create the excitement your story deserves better than you. After you are finished logging your video, this needs to be your first order of business. Write the anchor intro, and make it as good, punchy, and interesting as you can!

Remember how I keep harping on focus? The anchor intro helps you find the focus of your story quickly so you can narrow it down and get the perfect shots and write about just the best parts (not every single detail). When you sit down to write the anchor intro, it really forces you to find the best, most interesting, most important, and teasable part of your story. Also, once I've written the intro, I will go back and keep looking at it as I write my package to make sure I'm staying on track, staying true to my focus, and delivering on the promise that the anchor introduction makes.

There are times when you'll have to write the package first or it won't make air, but make it your general work routine to write the anchor intro first. It worked for me, and it will work for you.

LIVE REPORTER INTRO

This comes right after the anchor tosses it to you. If the anchor lead-in was to hook the viewer, the live reporter intro needs to set the hook. Remember, you're not simply repeating what the anchor said. Each story element needs to move the piece forward. Once again, like stand-ups, show viewers something. You're live out there for a reason, and you've hopefully put some thought into why you're there, so show the viewers. Small details work really great.

> *"Look, here is the bullet hole right by her window."*

> *"Here's the board that shows how many flights are delayed right now, look at all that red up there with few flights getting out on time."*

Think of this ten- to fifteen-second window as the chance for you to take the viewer to the heart of the story you've worked so hard to create, and write. Get viewers set and ready for the fabulous package you've prepared.

> *"And if you think this is bad, wait until you see what we found down the street."*

Bam! Who is going to change the channel? Set the mood for the package, keep building that excitement, and show viewers something from the scene.

PACKAGE

We've spent the whole chapter on this. This is the meat and potatoes. Let's tell the story here by revealing the emotion, human condition, and feelings you've worked so hard to uncover.

LIVE REPORTER TAG

Viewers just saw that great package. Was there anything you wanted to say that you didn't have video or time for? Now is the time to add that. What's next? Where can viewers get more information? What questions are still unresolved? Even better, what questions or concerns might viewers have after just watching your story? Now is the time to talk about it, but you don't have much time. This tag should also be ten to fifteen seconds.

ANCHOR TAG

There isn't usually an anchor tag after a live shot tag where I've worked, but maybe an anchor has a question for you. Or there's a website where viewers can get more information. This is the place for that. Or perhaps there's another story later in the newscast that is similar to this one or tied to it. This is where you or the producer can write something for the anchors to tease forward and let viewers know what to expect.

BEYOND THE BASICS

Beyond the basics, allow me to share a few tips or tricks that have really helped me in my storytelling. **Wayne's Top Ten Story Secrets:**

1. UNDERSTAND THE STORY.

There is nothing more important. No matter what it takes or who you have to speak with, make sure you understand the story. If you're confused about something, ask. There is nothing more frustrating than going to write a complicated story and realizing you don't really get it. The time to do so is the gathering phase. Don't be ashamed, or lazy, or shy about it. Do whatever it takes to make sure you get it. Because if you don't, you'll never be able to explain it to your viewers.

2. USE THE ONCE UPON A TIME METHOD.

This will SAVE you. If ever you feel like you just don't know where to start when you try to write your story, say to yourself, "Once upon a time…" and then start writing the first thing that pops into your head. That old fairy-tale beginning always got me to reset and uncomplicate matters so I could just drill down to the basics. *Once upon a time…* there was this coach who loved football and he was pretty good, but then this year was different because one of his players died in a car crash, and it totally changed the coach and his team.

EXAMPLE

Nat sound: whistle

Track: Every fall for the last ten years, you could find Coach Bill Masterson out here on the football field doing what he loved most.

SOT: "Football is my life."

Track: But this year, something has changed.

Saying "once upon a time" to yourself enables you to formulate a very condensed and simple version of your story. You'll be amazed with what then comes out when you then transfer that simplicity of thought into your script.

3. ALWAYS INTRODUCE YOUR MAJOR CHARACTERS.

This will instantly make your stories flow better, and it will allow the audience to meet your characters just as you did earlier in the day. It is so much better than just seeing a talking head pop out of nowhere with no reference.

Some reporters rely on the director to bring up the person's name and title at the right time, but that doesn't always happen. So, especially when you're doing a feature story or a story that has some heart to it, make sure you set up the person viewers are about to see with a one- or two-line introduction.

"One of the people here today to pay respects is Bill Johnson. We found him placing flowers

near the player's memorial. When we talked
to him, we learned why he felt he just had to
come here today."

Now viewers are paying more attention to what this man says. They watched him in action putting down flowers, they know his name, and now they're really curious what brought him out today. Much better than just popping him up out of nowhere.

You probably wouldn't want to do this with short MOS interviews or individuals you feel you don't need to feature (such as the teachers in the strike story), but if you're concentrating on someone, take the time to introduce them to viewers. Think of this as making an introduction.

4. PICTURE EVERY WORD YOU WRITE.

When you write a sentence down in your track, envision what video is going to go over your words. If there is no video that will fit, say something else (reword it). Think of the video you do have and reference it in some way to make your point. You can't change the shots, but you can change your words.

Stories are just flat out better if the words match the pictures. You don't have to describe each shot, but your words should complement the video as much as possible. Stories look unprofessional when it looks like the editor just put any old shots over the words to fill up the time. The easiest way to do this is to think about what shots you'll use to match the words you're about to write, almost like editing the piece in your mind. Trying to match them up after the fact is next to impossible.

5. LESS IS MORE.

I always tried to be clever, not wordy, when I wrote. Think about how to elicit emotion and feeling with short sentences (few words). You don't have to write flowery prose to turn a poignant phrase. I've always found that if you write directly, to the point, and set up your emotional soundbites, the result was very effective.

> *"It was on a Tuesday last month. Coach Masterson was sitting down to dinner with his family when he got the call that he'll never forget."*

Nothing flowery there, but it sets the stage for what we're about to hear. Write simply. Use short sentences. Make each word count.

6. WRITE IN ACTIVE, NOT PASSIVE, VOICE.

It's much more powerful, direct, and effective to write actively. That means always trying to start with the person or thing doing the action. The man robbed the bank (active) instead of the bank was robbed by the man (passive).

> The storm knocked out these windows.
> The wildfire tore through this community.
> The suspect shot the pedestrian.

You see passive writing in news. All. The. Time. It drives good writers crazy. Only after you get in the habit of writing actively can you break the rules when it makes sense to you.

If you're spending your day talking with a woman who got hit by a truck you might want to use the passive voice.

"And after she was almost home, after that long day at the hospital, she was hit by a truck just feet from her home."

Maybe the passive voice works just a bit better in that instance, but write in the active voice ninety-five percent of the time.

7. DON'T USE FALSE PRESENT.

I'm going to kick a hornet's nest here, but I *hate* false present. There are entire news networks built on using false present in their copy like: "A man running for cover," "Police racing to the scene," or "Onlookers diving under their tables." These are examples of reporters making something out to be happening now when it really isn't.

This is a very unnatural way to write and goes against my whole philosophy on writing and reporting, which is to write and talk like the audience. We do that so we can best reach and identify with them and vice versa. No one I know speaks in false present. "Hey, honey. Driving home now. Walking in door in thirty minutes and eating with you. Hoping you—bathing baby and walking dog earlier today is giving you a great appetite." Yet that's the way some stations and networks write their stories. Everything has an "ing" on the end...to add immediacy and drama, perhaps? I don't think so. False present is confusing, corny, and often sensationalizes something that isn't.

8. STAY AWAY FROM JARGON, POLICE SPEAK, AND CLICHÉS.

Jargon to me is any language that is specific to an industry, job, or hobby. It's an insider language. While it may sound like you're in the know using terms like that, why would you ever use them if your audience won't understand them?

Sometimes, reporters will use those words because they don't know what they mean and they literally can't translate that jargon into everyday language. Don't do that. Find someone who can explain what those terms mean, then use everyday terminology to convey the information. You'll understand the story better, and so will viewers.

The same goes for when you receive a press release or must work with an interview that uses police terminology. Let police officials say it, not you.

"The suspect entered the dwelling and retrieved a firearm," is just a fancy way of saying the man went into the apartment and came out with a gun. Remember, *you* should talk and write like a "real" person.

Last, clichés like "a bird in the hand," or "light at the end of the tunnel" can be overused. They're a crutch in your writing and should be avoided.

9. TAKE VIEWERS BY THE HAND.

This should really be your overarching philosophy. Think of yourself as a tour guide, there to guide viewers through all the important information. They know nothing and didn't spend all day learning about the topic of your story. They don't know the story subjects and may know next to nothing about the issue or location you're referencing. So make sure they don't get lost.

Take viewers by the hand—piece by piece, place by place—through your story and make sure you don't lose them along the way. It's your story, so you need to structure and write it in a way that makes it immediately understandable. That means it has a beginning, a middle, and an ending that makes sense, and the editing, shooting, and writing is not distracting.

10. HOW TO HANDLE SURPRISES AND DETAILS.

Everyone likes a nice surprise, and TV viewers are no different. Going back to our date analogy, when you look at a date across the table and say, "So it was a pretty average day until I went to park my car in the garage. Then something I never would have expected happened to me!" At that point, your date leans over the table, forgets about the menu, and locks eyes with you to find out what the heck happened.

You can use that when writing your story. Your best stories should have a twist or sudden, unexpected turn. Look for them as you work, and build them into your script. TV viewers are jaded. They know what formula reporters commonly use: "This happened. This person said this. Then this happened. Another person felt this way. And that's the end of the story." But if you can find the unexpected, surprise element you learned while out in the field, you can use that to create interest.

> *"After talking with a number of people at the fire shelter, we then found one family we just had to speak with. They brought something totally unexpected with them as they made their escape. Meet Rex. A twenty-five-pound goat, all curled up under this sleeping bag."*

Call attention to the unusual, and get the audience prepared to see it! Years later, people will still remember those surprising moments. "Hey, I remember when you found that goat at the shelter during that big wildfire!"

BONUS TIP

Finally, because you paid good money for my book, here's a bonus tip: **Good stories always have details.** I've told you before not to get caught up in numbers and obscure facts, but just a few details can make your story sing. That's where those close-up shots you got earlier come in handy. You got those shots because they were interesting. Now is the time to call attention to them in your script.

The ice dripping from the light fixture outside the barn, the rust flaking off the paint above the door handle on the old man's car, the signatures on the boy's arm cast as he lies in a hospital bed. Don't overdo it but do try to find these details in your story and then write about them. Bringing viewers very close to the story makes it more real and immediate for them. It becomes personal. They won't be able to look away, and you will have broken the barrier between the TV screen and the viewers' hearts. Doing that a couple of times a week will make you one of the best reporters in your market.

ONE MORE THING...

It's absolutely critical not to get yourself or your station sued. So stay tuned for some very important words about attribution.

That was a "deep tease" to get you to keep reading. Did it work?

EDITING

THIS WILL BE A SHORT CHAPTER since we're not going to get into the technicalities of editing. That's best taught by editing and photography experts. That's not me. However, I would like to offer a few words about editing for your consideration.

Stories can be wonderful or awful depending on how they're edited. I've had fabulous editors turn what I thought was going to be a ho-hum piece into a really great story, and I've had editors who didn't get what I was doing and turn a perfectly good piece into a bad one. It's that important.

To me, a well-edited piece comes down to pacing. An editor will make cuts and transitions to fit the mood of the story. The editing should not be distracting but complement the piece. Good editors are able to find the right flow, mix nat sound, and include the perfect pictures at the appropriate moments. It's also helpful to sit with the editor as they are working on the story so you can help them understand the mood you're looking for. You can be very clear with how you want the piece to look if you're in the room as it's being put together.

"No, it's okay, give it more room there."

"That pause is great! Don't feel like you have to jam everything together so fast."

"Keep that shot right there long...painfully long."

"Make us look at it."

If you're the one editing your own story, then you'll know what you're trying to accomplish, and you won't have to relay it to anyone. If you are working with a photographer who is also editing the story, hopefully you've talked all day about how you want this story to turn out. And because your shooter is editing the video they shot, they'll already know where the best shots are.

Be nice to editors. They are having to learn about your story from ground zero and all at once. Give them time to do a good job. If you put them under the gun day after day, they'll rightly take offense to that. Editors have to pay for all the wasted time in your day. They are the last people to work on the story, and they usually have the shortest time to do it. They are continually under deadline pressure. Be the reporter or MMJ who gives them time to do their important work. And if you're the editor, don't take for granted how crucial this step is. Allow yourself enough time to do it right.

EDITING TIPS:

- **START WITH NAT SOUND.** It's always best to start a piece with some type of natural sound, if possible. It sets the mood and gives the audience a chance to get ready to listen to your story. A short nat sound montage is also great.
- **SHOW ME A WIDE SHOT.** I like seeing a wide shot of the area within the first few seconds of the piece. I believe this helps orient the viewer to what we're about to see and where the story is set.
- **AVOID STARTING WITH STILL PICTURES OR GRAPHICS.** Starting the story with a graphic or a picture of someone or something is just kind of dead. There is no punch to the story with a silent opening.
- **IT'S OKAY TO START WITH A SOUNDBITE.** You can start your story with a soundbite as long as it's short. Then you introduce or explain who was talking. It's best if you can use the sound from the soundbite but show something else besides the person's mouth moving. But if you do start your story with a soundbite, and you can't see the person's mouth, that sound must be crystal clear.
- **VARIETY—MIX IT UP!** Hopefully you got all those different angles and shots for your story—wide, close-ups, high angle, low angle. Show them off in your piece instead

of all boring medium shots. And also try to have variety in how you start and end your stories. Don't get locked in and do the same techniques over and over again. Challenge yourself. It may not always work out perfectly, but it's fun to stretch your boundaries. Even with mistakes, you'll learn and improve. Don't be afraid to go for it! I've always felt it was easier to ask a reporter to dial it back a little than to have to push a reporter to try something new.

LIVE SHOTS

SO YOU WANT TO BE A LIVE SHOT HOTSHOT? Who doesn't? If you grew up with dreams of being a TV reporter, I'll bet that you practiced live shots as a kid in front of the mirror, holding a hairbrush as your microphone and tossing back to your favorite anchor person, either from a local channel or network. "Back to you, Kate!"

It's a great part of our job, and with new technology, we can do live shots from just about anywhere, anytime. You'll get a lot of practice doing live shots at your station, but if you're bad at them, you will be noticed for all the wrong reasons and may not be working there for long.

Also, because technology has made it easier to do live shots, some stations have forgotten about reporter safety, especially lone

MMJs. We'll address safety in a bit, but now let's concentrate on how to get comfortable doing live shots and how to improve what you're already doing. My suggestions can help you be better at live shots within a couple of weeks.

FRAME OF MIND—BREATHE!

When they toss to you in a live shot, you should be composed and comfortable but also have energy. Remember to breathe. Take your time. If you're new to live shots, of course you're going to be nervous. But use that nervousness to your advantage. Channel it into energy. The best way to do this is to concentrate, not on going live, but on being excited to tell everyone about your story. Make your story the thing to concentrate on. Relax, have fun, and have a simple conversation with the anchors about what you're seeing out there. Remember, you're only talking to one or two people. Pretend the camera is a person you know, and simply tell them what's going on.

USE YOUR ENVIRONMENT; SHOW VIEWERS SOMETHING!

Remember all the reasons I gave you earlier in the book for doing stand-ups: show-and-tell, time and location changes, etc.? These all make for great live shots. But remember, the best live shots aren't left to chance. You have to think about them from the moment you're handed your story assignment. Then as you're out covering the story, you should be thinking about what elements will give you the best backdrop or reason for a great live shot.

I know that many times we're so busy just getting the story written and edited that the live shot is wherever we can get a signal and be standing upright in time to toss to our story, but you're better than that. Throughout your day, you need to constantly evaluate where it would make the most sense to go live or what you could reveal, show, demonstrate, or interact with to make a great live shot. News management gets a bad reputation for making reporters go live just for the sake of doing so. Reporters believe that managers feel that the look of the live shot is more important than what's being said in the live shot. That might be somewhat true, but I always felt as a reporter that if the managers wanted me live in their show, then I had to think of a good reason to be live. It's not always possible, but have a good attitude and try to find the reason.

Show viewers something. (Are you tired of that phrase yet?) Start thinking about what would make a good live shot for your story at the beginning of your day, every day. And while there are some stories that absolutely should not have a live-shot component, it's hard to break producers of that habit because having a reporter live in your show does add energy and oomph to the newscast. Right or wrong, it just does. They get to break out the flashy graphics and the live banners, and it makes the show seem a bit more polished.

Do managers and producers go overboard in requesting live shots? Yes. Almost every day. Should you fight and ask not to do one when you feel it's just not appropriate? Yes. But you only get away with that so many times. I'm fine with you saying, this is a bad live shot story, but only after you've really thought about it and come up with reasons why it just won't work. Safety is not what we're talking about here, which is always a good reason not to do a live shot. More on that ahead. I'm talking about ideas. Try.

When you're scouting out a location to go live, you want a place where you can use your environment to further the story (something in that place will help your viewers understand or create interest in the story that's about to follow): near a thermometer inside of a ninety-five-degree apartment because they don't have air conditioning, on a bridge overlooking the massive tree that fell onto the interstate, the vending machine that dispenses Narcan meant to save the lives of overdose victims. The possibilities are endless, but many times, the backdrop to live shots just ends up being a building, police station, or hospital. Get creative and try to find something specific to *show viewers* during your live shot. Instead of standing in front of the fire station that responded to the fire, maybe ask if you can stand close to one of the trucks and tell viewers how many firefighters climbed on board to fight the fire. Be specific: more details make the shot more interesting. And don't wait until the last minute to figure it out.

FORGET MEMORIZING YOUR LIVE SHOTS

One of the reasons *why* people get so nervous for live shots is they are afraid they are going to forget what to say. Well, I don't think you should memorize your live shot! Whaaaaat?

In almost all the worst live shots I've ever seen, either the reporter forgot what they were going to say midstream, or they lost their place in a script, usually on their cell phone, and they didn't know what to do next. At that moment, your heart starts really beating hard, your brain is going a mile a minute, and you are supremely conscious of what an idiot you must look like in front of thousands of people.

Now understand, it seldom looks as bad as you think. Even if it did, so what? We all make mistakes. But I submit to you, this wouldn't happen if reporters didn't try to memorize their live shot. Trying to memorize a script is dangerous, especially when you're just starting, because one wrong word can knock you off track, and then it's hard to recover.

I always tried to avoid memorizing what I was going to say, but I did have a plan every time. I'd usually know where I wanted to start and where I wanted to end. And the plan worked well because all around me were visual cue cards to make sure I stayed on track.

You too, can use the "Garcia Method" for doing live shots. Once you've mastered it, you'll never go back, *and* your news director will be singing your praises. Rather than memorizing your live shot I want you to think of three bullet points that you want to get across and one or two elements you can physically show viewers in your live shot to represent those bullet points. Those elements you point at, walk toward, or have the camera move to, are the cue cards (visual references) that will help you remember what to say.

Say you're doing a story on that fire engine. You might start near the entrance to the garage, walk to show viewers the fire engine, and then point down to the hose while telling us how many gallons a minute it can pour on a fire. You'll remember all this because all you have to do is walk toward each item, and the item itself will remind you of what to say.

*"We're here at Station 51, which was the first
station to respond. Eight firefighters loaded
onto this fire engine right here, and it packs a
punch. As you see here, this hose was able to
put out ten gallons of water a second to stop
that fire from spreading."*

Easy, active live shot. You gave a behind-the-scenes look at one
of the tools that was used to fight the fire. And all you really had
to remember is, *I'm going to start outside here, move toward the
truck, and then bend down and show the hose to the camera.*

When you do have to memorize a script, say for a complicated
court case, I would highly advise you to write down your bullet
points, not the script. You'll be much more comfortable on air,
and you won't get lost. And, I know this sounds old-school, but if
you're really relying on notes, use a reporter's notebook and *not*
your cell phone. It's too easy to lose your place on a phone. Also,
someone could call or text or you, or you could accidentally hit
the screen and open another app. A notebook won't switch off
when you need it most.

Chances are your station will require you to send in a script for
approval that includes what you'll say in your live shot. You can
absolutely write it out and send it in, but I wouldn't worry about
repeating that script word for word when you go live. Bullet
points, walking and talking, and using objects as cue cards will
give you confidence and force you to be natural and conversa-
tional, which is what you should always be striving toward.

It may take a while to get this method down, and you may feel naked without your cell phone script, but this is the way to better performance.

If you're doing a live shot VO, or VO/SOT, then you'll most likely have to go by a script. That's fine. But I'd still suggest putting that script on a notepad and not on your cell phone.

RULE OF THREES

I don't know why I suggest making three points in live shots and stand-ups. It just works. The rule of threes: this, this, and that. Eggs, bacon, and toast. Hat, jacket, and scarf. It has an innate rhythm that resonates with people. It's not too little nor too much. Try it and see if you agree.

LOOK-LIVES

There will be many times you're asked to do a look-live instead of a live shot. It's basically the same thing, but you record it and edit it onto your package. Use the same techniques you would for a live shot, but don't ever say you're live when you're not.

HOW TO SHOOT LIVE SHOTS

If you're working with a good photographer, chances are at some point you're going to get some pushback about walk-and-talk live shots versus static ones where you stand in front of a building. Here's the deal: good photographers *want to make you look as good as possible.* And sometimes that involves putting up to five lights around you! If you're moving around, that makes it tough to light you. If they take the camera off the tripod to follow you around, the shot won't be as steady. So, their aversion to shaky, poorly lit shots is totally understandable. But you both must find a way to work together.

I felt the best way to work with photographers was to share my vision, and then leave it to them to figure out a way to pull it off. Most were good with that. And on those occasions where there wasn't a good reason to walk around, I was very happy for them to light me up and use every trick in the book to make me look good. I needed it! Just realize that you and the photographer may have different views about what a good live shot looks like. They are concentrating more on how it looks, you on what it says and how you say it. Compromise and work with that person.

SAFETY IS MOST IMPORTANT!

Make sure when going out live, you're always as safe as you can be. The two biggest threats to you are being run over by a car or truck and people who want to cause trouble. I think traffic can be a huge safety hazard to field crews, especially during live shots because you're forced to be in one place for a long time as you're setting up and waiting, and you're distracted.

We had a policy at the last station where I worked that we wouldn't let MMJs without photographers go live by themselves. There was no one to watch the MMJ's back. If you work at a station where they make you go live by yourself, pick as safe a spot as you can. Then do whatever you can to minimize the time you stand in front of the camera. Use your station vehicle as a way to shield yourself if possible. If you feel uncomfortable, let someone know. Don't be a hero.

Many times you'll be forced to broadcast on or near freeways. Make sure there is some kind of solid barrier between you and the lanes. Wear reflective clothing, do anything you can to be visible. Be conscious of your lighting so you don't blind or attract drivers.

Passers-by can also cause big problems for reporters going live. Just be aware of people around you, and always have a plan if something goes crazy. Let your producer know if someone may try to interrupt your live shot so they can be ready to jump out of your live shot and take your package if that happens. If I noticed a crowd of people standing around waiting for me to go live, I'd fake it five minutes early and act like I was live to see what they would do. If they started yelling, I'd act like I was doing my live shot, then pretend I was done (start to break down gear, etc.). They would usually leave. Then when my real live shot came up, I was good to go.

If you take anything from this section let it be this: If you feel unsafe at any point before or during a live shot, get out of there and let your station know as soon as you can. Hopefully you can alert them well before your live shot that the area is unsafe. You may have to cancel the live shot at the last minute. If your station faults you for that, it's on them. Frankly, you don't want to work for any employer that doesn't value your safety.

LET'S GET REAL

Will you always be able to think of those great, moving, show-and-tell live shots? No. But can you do it maybe half the time? I think that's a reasonable goal. If you do, you will get the reputation as someone who really goes the extra mile to reach out to viewers and make your stories and live shots interesting and memorable. Effort, attitude, and a willingness to not do it the way everyone else does it is all it takes. *How can I do this differently today?*

I'm aware that all good reporters have a go-to formula for banging out stories that are quick, efficient, and that works for them. But once you establish that routine, don't be afraid to mix it up. Try something totally different. Take a chance. That's what keeps you fresh and keeps the job interesting.

BONUS TIP

There was a point in my career when I went from being just okay to being pretty good at doing live shots. It involved an attitude shift.

I always felt I was just a small cog in the big wheel of a newscast. And perhaps I didn't feel that I was as good as everyone else who appeared in that newscast, especially the very seasoned anchors. Subconsciously, I think I just wanted to get my live shot done and go home without screwing up.

Then one day it hit me. Just as the anchors really take ownership of their newscast (as they should), I decided my two or three minutes was just as important. And from that point on, when the anchors tossed to me, I made it *my* segment. My mindset was I really had something important to tell viewers, and I spent all day working on it. No one knew *my* story better than I did. I just took ownership of that time in the newscast and made it MINE! That mental shift in how I looked at my time in front of the camera really made a difference for me and gave me real confidence. It caused me to take my time and not rush, feeling that what I was saying was every bit as worthwhile as anything else in the newscast.

Own your live shots and that block of time they give you each day. You can do anything you want with those precious few minutes. Make them memorable, interesting, and appropriate to the story. You're worth it! You can be every bit as captivating as the anchors, maybe even more so because you're showing us something and you have an environment out there to work with. You can do it!

ANCHORING

AS MUCH TIME AS I SPENT REPORTING, and it feels like a lifetime, I actually have more years under my belt as an anchor. I'm going to share with you some tips I know will help you if you ever get called in by the boss to fill in or if you get that promotion to weekend anchor. First, let's go over the basics.

Is anchoring better than reporting? No. Anchoring is not better than reporting. It's different than reporting. Here is how I see the two positions:

ANCHORS

Better Pay

*Better Working Conditions

*More Overall Pressure

*More After Work Commitments

*Immersed in Station Politics

*Very Strict Dress Code

*Never Really Off

REPORTERS

*More Exciting

*More Job Security

*More Likely to Have a Day Shift

*More Daily Pressure

*More Dangerous

*Very Tough Working Conditions (Rain,
Snow, Smoke, No Restrooms)

It's no secret that main anchors at TV stations are among the most highly paid employees. However, anchors in less-watched time slots aren't paid as well. Generally though, all anchors will almost always make more money than reporters because they will usually have more experience and hopefully already gained that valuable experience as a previous reporter. The jobs are very different. Reporters are sent into the wind to gather and present one or two stories. Anchors stay in the studio and are tasked with presenting *all* the stories contained in the newscast. Sometimes anchors will be asked to write packages, or in smaller markets, may be asked to spend part of their day reporting in the field.

Anchors who aren't asked to report aren't under the same kind of daily deadline pressure that reporters and MMJs face. Their pressure is different—coming from ratings and bosses who will look to fire anchors first when stations don't perform well, whether it's an anchor's fault or not. Anchors are judged daily by managers and especially the audience, who will not hesitate to pounce on any flaw whether it's a mispronunciation, ugly tie, or a dress that some viewers may feel "shows too much," or is "unprofessional."

Longtime anchors' value in a market increases along with experience and face and name recognition. But that also means they always have to be on. Viewers will approach anchors at the grocery store and act as if they know them personally because in their minds, they do. And that's really the goal. As an anchor you want to feel connected, recognized, and feel as if viewers know you, even if they only see you through a TV screen. Even if you've never seen them before in your life, they see you almost every night.

This comes with the territory, and anchors must remember to be polite and respectful at all times. With the prevalence of cell phones, one wrong step could get your face blasted all over social media in the worst way and could result with you losing your job. As a TV journalist, don't ever pull the, "Don't you know who I am?" card. Also, be careful of accepting favors, which we'll address later in the Ethics and Attribution chapter.

As an anchor, especially in smaller markets, everyone will be watching what you do—getting sloppy drunk at the bar, yelling at a barista, whether you pick up trash in your neighborhoods while you walk, or if you are nice to your dog. The good *and* the bad are amplified. It's also important to avoid getting into trouble with the law. A drunk driving arrest is not only careless and thoughtless, but it can end a career for someone in TV news. And the public's memory, of good and bad events can last a long, long time.

Let's now discuss the job itself. Generally, the highest-paid anchors will either work the early-morning shift or the late-night shift.

Working early mornings means getting up at 2:30 or 3:00 a.m. to get to the station, put on makeup, wake up (not necessarily in that order), and be totally ready to go when the show open hits.

Working nights means getting to work around 3:00 p.m. and working through the last newscast of the night (an early evening newscast or two then the late show). When I anchored, my shows were an hour at 4:00 p.m., an hour at 8:00 p.m., an hour at 10:00 p.m., and a half hour at 11:00 p.m. If someone was on vacation or sick, I'd have to pick up another hour or two. That's a lot of talking.

Chances are, those just starting to anchor newscasts will begin their career anchoring weekend mornings, which is the same as weekday mornings except the shows are generally shorter and more understaffed.

There are rare times when one or two anchors at a station will work bankers' hours. They typically start anchoring a lifestyle show at 10:00 a.m., the noon news, then maybe an early-evening newscast, and call it a day. Even though the hours are great on this shift, it's not usually given to the top anchors at a station, and it doesn't pay as well due to viewership levels. There just aren't as many people watching television during the day because they are at work, school, or doing other things. Viewership levels have changed in the time since I first started anchoring. It used to be nights were the big newscast (the 10:00 p.m. or 11:00 p.m. news), but now in most markets, morning viewership has eclipsed night newscasts. So many stations have not only put their top talent on the morning shows, but they've expanded morning news hours so they can sell more commercials.

What this means is that if you want to make the transition from reporter to anchor, to really make it in this business you'll either be working at the crack of dawn or at night. Either shift can have a major effect on raising a family. Will you be okay with working a morning shift where your spouse has to get your kids off to school, and you're bone tired at 7:00 p.m.? Or are you good with seeing your kids only in the morning if you work nights? Your personal commitments should be a consideration when pursuing an anchor position.

Before we get into more specifics of the job, I want to talk about job security. Most places I've worked, reporters and MMJs were way down on the list of being fired when new owners or management took over. As long as you do your job and keep your head down you are relatively safe (except in the cases of big corporate mergers when everyone is on the chopping block). Anchors, however, are always some of the first to be let go when ratings are down.

It always struck me as strange that anchors should take the blame when things go badly but are rarely given credit when things go well. It's all about the content, breaking news, and weather when ratings are great, but when the ratings tank, interestingly, management doesn't blame the content but instead looks to change the anchors.

The only position more dangerous than anchor in the newsroom is the news director. If a station sinks from first to third, or stays third or fourth for years, station managers often look to make a change with the person in charge of the department. It's actually very similar to sports teams. First to go are coaches after a bad season. If the team is playing badly, next in line is the quarterback who's just not living up to expectations. Never mind his offensive line is a wreck and he gets sacked all the time. So just know if you choose to go down the anchor path, there will always be pressure on you, especially if you're working for the number-three- or four-rated station in the market. During much of my career, I was very lucky to be working at the top one or two stations, and as long as we were winning, they left me alone. I have no doubts what my fate would have been had we slipped.

THE JOB

A reporter's job is to communicate one story to the viewers. An anchor communicates *all* the stories to the viewers. That means making every story they read their own and applying the same ownership a reporter gives a story they've worked on all day to *every* story in the newscast. That's the goal, anyway.

Anchors need to instantly set the correct tone for each story of the newscast and to make sure every script makes sense and is written in a way that is comfortable to read. It means going through scripts and making sure they know how to pronounce all the words that will appear on the prompter, including names of people and places they may have never heard before. And even when they do their due diligence and go over all names with a fine-tooth comb, they'll still make mistakes.

I've found there will always be words you "thought" you knew how to pronounce, but whoops…no. Most of the times I screwed up a word, it was one I didn't even think to ask about because it seemed so obvious. Who knew in the Portland area the street Couch is pronounced Kooch? Or that Aloha High School with the mascot of Rainbow Warriors is pronounced uh LOW uh and not uh LOW hah as they'd say in Hawaii?

Besides being on the air and communicating stories, anchors are also a link between management and other newsroom workers. Managers will sometimes use anchors as sounding boards to see how a new policy might be received by the staff.

I think anchors should be a two-way conduit between management and the rest of the staff. What I mean by that is that if there is something that's really bugging the staff, anchors are the ideal person in the newsroom to take it into the news director's office and present it in a way that will give the best chance to improve the situation. Anchors aren't usually managers, so people usually feel more open to discussing problems with them than they would with a direct supervisor. And anchors are usually closer to news managers than other employees, so they can in essence mediate newsroom problems and offer solutions that make both sides happy.

A good anchor will be someone both a news director and a prompter operator can take into their confidence and know the information will be safe. The best anchors are not tattletales; they are problem solvers and will constantly work to improve morale and the working environment at a station.

Your attitude is extremely important as an anchor. Whether you know it or not, many employees (and managers) will see you as the face of the station. Maybe some of them grew up watching you. Maybe you got the anchor job they wanted. They all think you are paid well and highly respected so they will look to you for not only your story judgments but also how you function in the workplace. If you have a great attitude, walk into the station upbeat and positive, genuinely greet producers and others and listen to them, you can have a huge impact on morale and creating a positive station culture. Let me repeat that. **You, solely by your position as an anchor, can greatly affect the working environment around you!**

Unfortunately, the reverse is also true. If you come into the station late, grouchy, complaining about misspellings or words missing in scripts (that really you were supposed to catch before air), or if you hide in an office all day and give off the vibe that you'd rather be somewhere else, that also can have a huge effect on creating a negative atmosphere in the newsroom. Trust me. Workers will follow your lead. You, even more than managers, help set the expectations of the average worker since you're one of them and you spend your shift with them. Don't gripe all the time about the quality of the newscast if you're not happy with it. If you're that disgusted, do something about it. Get in and work and help. Everything you do as an anchor is magnified. So why not be a positive force and make everyone's lives better? I know you will.

Another important function of anchors is being the station's representative at charity and business events. Perhaps the station has a new big client they are trying to woo. A main anchor might be asked to meet that potential advertiser at a luncheon or hang out in the box suite at a concert or football game. I think this is a huge compliment and it is a sure sign that you are on good terms with your management team. Does it cut into your free time? Sometimes. But in the end, I think it's worth it. You also may be asked to host charity events. If it's a station partner, you know you'll be providing a service to the charity and your boss. And again, it shows your value to the station. It's even something you can mention when it's time to negotiate your next contract. There may be other charities out of the blue that may ask you to work with them at a fundraiser. My station always encouraged this because it got us out into the community and exposed us to potential new viewers. Plus, it was just a good thing to do to help the community.

Sometimes a charity would offer to pay me for my services, but I never accepted any payments. You may, and that's fine. But my advice is to always check with your news director before you agree to get involved with any outside public activity or accept any payment or favors. And you should do your homework to make sure the group asking you to help won't bring any controversy to your station.

HOW TO ANCHOR

Alright. Let's finally drill down into what you need to know to anchor a newscast. I've compiled this little Wayne's List that you've seen in other parts of this book, so why not continue the trend? Here are ten points to help you along as you anchor a newscast. This will help if you're a first-time anchor or have been doing it for a while. Remember these are not commandments. They are suggestions.

1. BE INTERNALLY CALM.

This was always hugely important for me and the foundation for everything I did. If I was nervous or angry, I couldn't reach my full potential as an anchor. I couldn't think or concentrate (a bad combination for a news anchor). So while you want to be energetic and dynamic as an anchor, internally you want to be rock steady and calm. Realize that this is just a job, like any other. Breathe. Try to block out all the lights and cameras and remember your true mission: to communicate information to your "audience of one." Visualize them at home and talk to them. What also helped me relax was knowing that if I made a mistake, it wasn't the end of the world.

2. BE RESPECTFUL.

I always respected my viewers. They were doing me a favor by watching me! I felt they were loyal to me, and I wanted to be loyal to them by being honest, not wasting their time, not scaring them, teasing them, or talking down to them. Instead, I treated them like friends. I always considered it a privilege to be invited into their homes, and I wanted to behave like a good guest.

If you have the mindset that your viewers deserve the best information and your best as an anchor, you'll have a solid career in journalism. If you think of viewers as allies, you'll demand better stories, more honest teases, and when everyone wants to hype up a nonevent, you'll be the calm voice of reason in the room saying, "Let's play this straight. Let's inform, not scare." Or the opposite could happen. Maybe there is a big story that could really affect your viewers but no one else is interested. "We have to get this on the air and make a big deal about it!" People will listen to you.

Being respectful is more than your actions. To me it's a mindset, an attitude, and even a philosophy that will help guide you when having to make difficult decisions.

3. BE YOURSELF.

Easier said than done. But of all the points on here, this may be the most important. This is the acquired talent that takes you from an average anchor to a very good one. It's when you can block out all that crap in the studio and become totally at ease and comfortable and just tell us what's going on. I'll be honest. There are very, very few people who can do this without lots and lots of time on the desk. It just takes hours and hours of doing it before it becomes no big deal and second nature. But it's when you stop trying to be an anchor, when you stop trying to read the news like someone else you've admired, when you stop being on guard and fearful of mistakes, that's when you really begin to connect with the audience. Find your own style. Don't be like someone else. Be you. A respectful you! Had to throw that in. But you know what I mean. You can't imitate anyone as well as letting the real you shine through. And why is it important? Because I truly believe the audience can tell. They know when someone is faking it and when they are genuine. Again, I trust the viewers. They really do know.

4. COMMUNICATE.

We've hit on this so many times you're probably done with me. But it's so important. At the end of the day, whether you're a reporter or anchor, all you really need to do is communicate. Tell me the story in a way that makes me understand it, and if possible, care. That's it. That is the heart of everything.

Again, my technique is to pretend I'm talking to my wife or a friend. That's exactly the way you need to think. Tell me what happened in your own way, with your own words, in a way that is meaningful to you. If you find a way to care about each story, or at least some of the stories, you'll make me, the viewer care, too.

Communicating, I think, is much easier for reporters because they've spent the day on their story. They know it inside and out and have had time to really sink their teeth into it. But as an anchor you must feel that way about every story. You really need to own every story that passes from your lips so that you can truly tell the viewer about it. It's not easy and you won't be able to do that with every story, every day. But that's the goal.

5. BE READY FOR ANYTHING.

This is where anchors earn their money. When everything goes wrong, you must be able to think of something intelligent to say and keep the show going. "That sounds great, Wayne, but how exactly am I supposed to do that?" Well first, by being prepared. If you have to run your own prompter or if someone else does that for you, the most common problem that will really throw an anchor is when out of nowhere the prompter stops working. That can be caused by any number of issues. The important thing is that you always have a backup. In the old days we used to have a telephone book-size stack of paper scripts. And even though you were mostly reading from the prompter, we anchors had a knack of being able to keep the scripts on our desk in sync with where we were in the newscast. So if the prompter went down, it would only take a second or two to find your place in the paper script.

However, in the last few years, most stations have eliminated paper scripts so we've only had our computers to rely on if something went wrong. That's fine, but again, you have to make sure you keep your place on the computer in case the prompter dies. When that happens, don't panic, just read slowly, describe what you see on the TV monitor if you have to, until you can find your place.

The worst is when the prompter dies when you are on camera. Because then the viewers can see you scrambling to find your place on the computer. But again, don't panic. You can even say, "Just give me a second to find my place here." Be transparent. Don't be embarrassed. Just get the show back on track as soon as you can. There have been many times when a show was melting down and a producer wasn't talking to me and I said out loud on the air, "Okay, what story are we doing now?" And believe me your producer will answer you then. And then you move ahead and keep going. When all else fails, toss to weather! Just make sure you do it slowly, so you give your weather person time to put down the ice cream cone and get their computer graphics ready.

You don't always have to call attention to mistakes unless they are extremely obvious. And if that's the case don't throw anyone under the bus. Just apologize and ask for a little time to get things straightened out.

When a show is in meltdown mode because of a failed live shot, technical problems, or whatever, just know this is your chance to manage the disaster. This is actually an opportunity for you. Be calm, be respectful, and just get through it. It might look ugly, but hey, it's TV news, and the awkwardness will be over soon.

6. WORKING WITH CO-ANCHORS.

You may not be alone out there on the set, and most times that's a good thing. A good co-anchor can help pump you up when you're down and can save you during breaking news as you take turns thinking of things to say. One of you can look up facts on the web, the other can carry the conversation on the air, and then you switch.

Having a co-anchor can add fullness to your performance and to the show as a whole. The key is having a real, authentically good relationship with your co-anchor. It takes years sometimes to get into the flow where you know what the other is going to say. I do think viewers can tell when you're faking it. And I think you really have to like each other off camera or be friends, which is not always possible.

What is important to get straight right from the get-go is that you are equals but you don't have to be the same. It's always better when co-anchors have different strengths, interests, and even styles. Viewers should feel comforted watching you both on TV, not sensing stress or underlying tension. So even if you don't get along off camera, make an effort and come to an agreement to have a good relationship on camera.

I had the great pleasure of having about eight great co-anchors in my career. They were all a little different, and I loved that. I always tried to avoid comparing anchor to anchor and just enjoyed each of them for what they brought to the table. But one thing I always worked hard at was to make sure they felt they knew they didn't have to answer to me about anything. And if producers gave me too many reads in a show or had me read the lead story a few days in a row, I called attention to that to make sure my co-anchor was getting equal treatment.

When you have a great relationship with your co-anchor, work is just more fun. The best part of my job was going to work and sitting down next to friends for a few hours every day. They will be the people you spend the most time with during your entire week.

The other thing I tried to make clear with my co-anchors was that I always had their backs. Partly because of the time spent together, partly because of the similar jobs and expectations, you should have no closer work relationship than your co-anchor. There's no room for jealousy or pettiness or gossip or any other destructive behaviors that could damage your relationship. Treat your co-anchor with respect, and hopefully the feeling will be mutual, and you will have an important, unshakable ally at work. The station will also have a winning team that viewers will make an effort to watch.

When you're anchoring breaking news, or unscripted events with a co-anchor, you need to talk and hash out a plan before you go on the air. Use paper and pen and work out who will start, who will toss to the reporter, and who will read what. Very basic, but it's always best to have some kind of a game plan. It eliminates the awkwardness. When you work with someone for years, you can just give them a look and they'll know what the plan is. That's when the magic happens and you're so happy to have someone by your side during the stressful moments. But until you have that kind of relationship, don't be afraid to talk and ask questions and work it out before the red on-air light goes on.

7. CROSS TALK.

I suppose this is as good a time as ever to talk about cross talk (chit-chat) at the anchor desk. It should be kept to a minimum, especially when you're first starting or filling in. Unless you have the perfect thing to say, and maybe even if you have the perfect thing to say, just don't. Go on with the newscast. So many things can go wrong with ad-libbing or making snide on-air comments after a story. You could show your bias, you could make a silly joke that takes away from the story, or more likely you'll say something that is just unnecessary and a time waster that turns out to be not as clever as you'd hoped.

Some news directors will say absolutely no cross talk, but I think that's misguided, too. Once you have some experience under your belt, a comment here and there adds a human dimension and shows your personality during the newscast. Many times, your comment might echo a question or feeling your audience might have after watching. What I'm saying is, less is more.

Think of it like a dinner party with a group of people who all know each other but you're the stranger. Observe, be polite, don't stick your neck out. Once you've been there a while you can start to open up on the air and you'll be able to spot opportunities to share. But remember it is much harder to stick your foot in your mouth when it's closed. I think a pause, or a subtle reaction with your eyes after a particularly sad or emotion evoking story is far more effective in conveying humanity to the viewer than an offhand comment.

And here's one more big tip in reacting to those stories from the desk. Begin your tag or reaction while you're looking at the monitor, and then slowly as you're talking, turn toward the camera. That way, viewers feel as though you've watched the story with them and you don't look like a deer in the headlights waiting for the tally (red on-air light) light to come on while staring straight at the camera. In fact, don't be afraid at any point while you're on camera to look or glance at the monitor. Just do it casually, and don't hide it. And do it slowly like you mean it; don't jerk back and forth. There were many times when we were in two boxes (a split screen with a reporter and anchor on either side) where I'd look at the monitor instead of the camera so I could see what the reporter was saying and their expression. That's totally fine in my book. Just make sure the monitor is fairly close to the camera and not way to one side or the other.

8. ELECTIONS, BREAKING, AND EVENTS.

There may come a time when you are asked to anchor live coverage of an event. That might be a parade, or an election, or even extended breaking news. The best advice for you is to prepare as much as you can. If you're doing an election, find out what races will be most prominently featured on your newscast and get to know the issues. Make a cheat sheet to have on set that gives a one-line description of each candidate, location of districts, and ballot measure definitions. These have to be simple because you won't have more than a few seconds to explain them as the different races go cycling by on the screen.

For major races do a more extended biography of the major candidates so you can talk at length about each of them as you're going live to the campaign headquarters and having to fill time before they get to the microphone to give their speeches.

For elections, preparation is key. Spend at least a couple of days getting to know the issues, the pro and con arguments, and on election night, be prepared to lay them out if need be. But be careful. Just as we talked about with reporting, simplicity is key.

Just because you collected all this information doesn't mean you necessarily have to share all of it. Don't force it. If an opportunity arises to use it, go ahead. But don't hold up the show because you're spouting off facts.

During events or parades, make sure you keep a close eye on the on-air monitor. This will be your guide for what to talk about. If a float with the queen is going by on the screen, you don't want to be talking about a marching band. It seems so elementary, but you'd be surprised. Address what's on the screen, whether it's a fire, crash, fireworks going off, or a cute baby. Also if the image or person on the screen changes, that's your cue to quickly wrap up your thoughts and move on to the next subject.

There's obviously very little preparation you can do for breaking news, unless it's a drawn-out affair or you're coming in to relieve another anchor who's been on the desk all morning. In that case (and in any breaking news case) it's vital to make a little cheat sheet for yourself with where the crews are located and what they are covering. Maybe Betty is at an evacuation shelter at a high school gym, Pete is on the fire lines on the edge of another town, and Mary is at the incident command post at city hall. It's very important you know where everyone is so you can quickly toss to them without needing someone to write you an intro. Because there will be no time. The producer may simply say to you, "Hey, go to Betty after this VO," so you'll need to know where she is and what angle she's covering.

Again, watch the screen because they may tell you you're going to toss to Betty, but then Pete pops up. Well, sometimes plans change, so be flexible and don't get angry or call attention to the mistake by saying, "Well, I thought we were going to Betty, but here's Pete." Just go with it as if it was the plan all along. Keep your head, concentrate, and listen! If there are any questions you have during Pete's report, don't be afraid to tell the producer you want to ask a question after Pete wraps up. If you were wondering about something, chances are the audience was as well.

In all these situations, the monitor is your friend. Keep a close eye on it, and know at all times what your audience is looking at. Try to explain the pictures and scenes they are seeing.

9. DELIVERY AND DYNAMICS.

As you know by now, my whole philosophy about being a TV journalist centers around relating to your audience. Writing like them, talking like them, anticipating their concerns, questions, what they might find humorous, interesting, sad, or shocking. So when you sit down at the anchor desk, keeping all that in mind, just tell me the news. In your own way. Be yourself.

One of the biggest mistakes I see from inexperienced anchors is that they are so caught up in not making mistakes that they forget to be real people up there. Let me clue you in on a little secret: It's way more important to communicate the story and be real than it is to be a machine who never flubs a script. Read that again before you move on. It's okay to not be perfect.

You ever have a conversation with someone and get tongue-tied or slur a phrase? Of course. Does the person you're talking to make you stop and say, "Hey, you really messed up that word."

If anything, you both laugh at your mistake. Flubbing up words once in a while is just a part of how we talk to each other. So understand mistakes may happen on the air, but it's okay as long as you get the point of the story across.

Clearly, you don't want to flub up more than a couple of times a newscast, but it will happen from time to time. Don't beat yourself up over it. Move on. Don't be so bent on perfection that you start to worry about every little mistake you make. That will only ruin your confidence.

When I anchored and made a mistake, I pretended it never happened and wouldn't think of it again. I think that really helped me. It's like a relief pitcher who gives up a home run but still has to pitch the rest of the game. You've got a job to do out there, too. Don't let a mistake or two derail the newscast or make you worry about how you'll perform tomorrow. Again, I'm talking about speech flubs here. Obviously if you accidentally say something that's inaccurate or wrong, that kind of mistake needs to be corrected immediately.

Remember what I said before. Every day is a new day. If you were great, so what? You'll have to prove yourself all over again tomorrow. If you stunk it up, so what? You'll get a chance to do better tomorrow.

Now let's talk about what I think makes a good anchor in terms of delivery, pacing, and range. I believe that one of the worst things you could do as an anchor is deliver every story the same way. You might say, "But, Wayne, that means I'm being consistent and smooth." Nope. Again, think about how we talk to each other. Sometimes you're excited and talk fast. Sometimes you whisper. Sometimes you emphasize something and talk slowly. Sometimes you raise your voice. Well, we should anchor the same way. The only difference is you probably need to add a bit more energy than you normally would if you're just talking to your friend. You need to speak a little more clearly than normal, and you can't cuss or say offensive things. So it's still you out there on the anchor desk, but maybe you've just cleaned it up a little. Make sense?

Let's look at it another way. Have you ever seen those EKG readouts when they do tests on hearts? You know how the line goes up and down and up and down. I think your anchoring should be like that in terms of range, speed, intensity, loudness, etc. There should be diversity.

In any given newscast you'll have hard news, sad stories, funny stories, shocking stories, and once in a while, stories that will leave you stunned. It's okay to show that while you're anchoring because your tone helps communicate the story to the viewer. The way you talk, your smile or frown, a raised eyebrow or look from your eyes can be just as powerful in communicating as the words you read. I'm not saying to be biased and to subtlety tell the audience how to feel about a controversial topic, but I'm saying to be human! When you come across an obviously sad story, it's okay to sound sad. It's okay to be happy if a local kid won a spelling bee competition. What's not okay is to be a robot who reads everything the same. If the story is exciting or dangerous, talk fast and be intense with a lot of energy. If you're reading a story that is really heart wrenching, it's okay to pause for a second or even two after you read the hardest part. **Pauses are among the most effective tools an anchor can use to convey emotion.** Use it once in a while and you'll see that I'm right. Force yourself to be quiet for a beat longer than you think you should. It really serves to emphasize what you just told us.

10. HUMBLE YET CONFIDENT.

You can take it or leave this advice, but I always thought the combination that worked for me as an anchor was to be humble, yet confident. You don't have to be the smartest person in the room. It's okay to say, "I didn't know that," or, "I don't know the answer to that, but I'm going to find out." I always thought that I connected better to viewers when I showed I was one of them, was truly interested in what we were telling them, and I felt they would be too. As an anchor, I never felt I had to get the last word in. I never felt I had to always say goodbye too if my co-anchor already said it. Take each day as it comes. Be humble yet confident on and off the set. Be a good person. Be human.

When you get comfortable, don't be afraid to be vulnerable or show weakness. Those qualities help viewers see the real you and when they connect with you they will watch. Our flaws aren't always a negative. They help us become a three-dimensional person in a two-dimensional medium. Embrace the good and the imperfections in you. Always try to get better but enjoy the journey getting there.

BONUS: THE MICROPHONE IS ALWAYS HOT.

As a reporter, and especially as an anchor, always know that your microphone is (or could be) on, and anything you say could accidentally get on the air. And realize if you're in a studio, even if you don't have a microphone on, others might. So just make it your personal policy now and forever that whenever you have a microphone clipped on, you're holding one, or you're near one, if you have to speak, do so as if you're already on air. I've seen reporters mess up a prerecorded look-alive or stand-up and then say something bad or curse thinking it would never be on the air. Well, some editor was in a hurry and picked the wrong shot to throw on a package, and presto! Someone is in big trouble.

Your microphone can also pick up comments when you complain or gossip about co-workers. The people in the control room can hear you, managers can go back later and listen in if your station is like most and digitally records everything that passes through the studio. So microphone or not, if you have something negative to say, it's best to save it for the right time, not while everyone (including possibly the viewers) is listening in. It's like an email or text. They can easily wind up in the wrong hands, so be careful.

SOCIAL MEDIA

THERE CAN BE LITTLE DOUBT that if you're going to be a TV journalist in today's world you'll also have to be proficient in many aspects of social media. That means posting to social media sites like Twitter (X), Facebook, Instagram, TikTok, etc., and your own station's website and/or social media accounts. Some of this may come easier to younger reporters who grew up with social media and know how to use these accounts to their advantage.

Still, I hope you'll think about the few words of advice I'm about to impart. The best time to begin thinking about your social media presence is before you even apply for your next TV job. If you haven't already done so, do a search on Google of yourself, as any good employer will do, and see what turns up. Go through your personal accounts and text streams and take a hard look at what you've posted and texted from an employer's/viewer's perspective. Determine whether your words and photos represent the person you want to project to your prospective new bosses. Trust me, someone will eventually look.

I'm not a prude by any means, but if you are deeply opinionated on controversial topics, use a good deal of foul language, or post numerous revealing pictures of yourself, you might want to seriously edit your accounts. Even then, you may not be safe if someone took a screenshot of your posts or texts.

Employers, especially in the field of journalism, are looking for professional people who keep their biases to themselves. When you're a journalist, your job is to be open to all sides and then present the facts. If your heels are already dug in on an issue, or it appears they are, employers will have concerns about your ability to be fair.

You may say, well, what about transparency? Yes, transparency is important, but news employers have to trust you to keep your own feelings out of the story and be fair. If your Instagram is full of one-sided political posts, that will be a red flag to employers. So you have to decide which is more important: your career or editorializing on social media. I'm just laying out the truth; you decide what to do with it.

During your first interview with a potential station and again on your first day of actual work, you should sit down with your manager and be clear on what the expectations are for social

media. Where I worked, we didn't really have a policy or specific demands on where and how often you should post on
social accounts. But there were expectations that we'd write a
story each night for the web about the story we covered on air.
That's why it's important to get those expectations on record at
the very beginning.

It's reasonable that reporters and MMJs be asked to be active
on at least one of the social media sites and own that one. Your
boss might have a favorite, but we all gravitate toward the one
that best suits our style and personality. Whichever you choose,
try to get in the habit of posting every workday. Be careful with
your posts so that you're not tipping off the competition. Believe
me, they'll be monitoring. And if it's early enough in the day,
and you're on a good story, they won't be above switching their
reporter to cover what you've been posting about.

Breaking news is different. I would post early and often about
where you're going and what you're seeing and include video
and photo snippets. Your station can lift these media files and
use them on the air, or your main station account can repost
them to their larger audience.

Posting also immediately tells your producers what you're
working on, where you're going, and what you're seeing. If you
get in the habit of posting on social media, you may even be
able to dispense with having to call or email the newsroom
(they can all just read your posts). But, just as you would for
air, make sure these posts are accurate, that you're not guess-
ing, and that you're just describing what you're seeing or what

an official source is telling you, and name that source. You don't want folks to screenshot an erroneous post and use that against you later. You will find out in breaking news situations that information you may think is solid turns out later to be wrong. So be general (just as I suggested in the Breaking News chapter). "I'm on my way to a fire in downtown, and as you can see in this photo, smoke is visible from the east side," not, "I'm hearing this fire was started by a group of cub scouts, and I'm going to check if that's true."

Just realize your professional social media accounts are a reflection of you. When viewers see you on TV and are interested in you, they'll seek you out on social media and follow you. When I was on the air, I would always include personal posts about what I was doing, eating, where I was going, who I was meeting, etc. but not too much. Every couple of days, I'd post just enough to give viewers a glimpse into my life so they could see me as a real person.

I also think it's very important that when you post you are engaging politely with folks, like their replies, etc. I think reporters and anchors who only post to drive traffic to a promotion or station web story are really missing the point. All your posts should not be asking the viewer to do something for you or for you to promote the station. Viewers will discount you if all you do is sell, sell, sell. Show something of yourself—as much as you feel comfortable. And don't use your station media account to blast people or companies that may have wronged you. It's not a good look when you use your media power to browbeat a company when average viewers can't do that.

And while we're on the subject of bad looks, never post happy pictures at scenes of tragedies. This should go unsaid, but I've seen reporters at the scene of a shooting posting pictures of themselves smiling in front of the police tape. Be aware of what you post and how it might be perceived. Before you hit post, think, *Would anyone have a problem with this?* If so be safe and don't post it.

So with that, let me give you Wayne's Top Five Rules for Social Media Accounts:

1. DON'T EMBARRASS THE STATION.

This may seem obvious, but don't post something that could reflect negatively on the station.

2. DON'T EMBARRASS YOURSELF.

Your personal brand is worth something, and its value increases the longer you're in this business. Don't ruin it by posting something that will reflect negatively on you. You may be very tempted to weigh in on controversial topics, but don't. You're not going to change any minds, and you will lose followers.

Also, don't engage in fights with followers. Block them, ignore them, report them to your boss, but DO NOT give them the satisfaction of engaging with them, publicly or privately. Remember, everything you write—whether it's on a public forum, in a private message, or in an email—can be used against you. Every time you respond to someone on social media, imagine if the contents were made public and whether you'd be okay with that. Would your boss be okay with that? When you repost someone's negative comment about you, or even reply, you are literally giving that person the attention of your entire audience that you worked so hard to assemble. Don't share that power and attention with someone who is being a jerk!

3. INFORM THE PUBLIC.

Let the public know about the important news you're covering and how it affects them with photos, video, short stand-ups, etc. Make your account valuable to the people in your community!

4. ENGAGE THE PUBLIC.

Treat your followers as real people and take an interest in what they have to say. Answer their questions if you can and address their concerns in a respectful way. Don't treat them like a number. Take an interest in some of your most loyal followers, but make sure you don't cross the line from an online conversation to an in-person meetup. That can be dangerous. If you sense danger from one of your online followers, trust your gut.

5. SHOW YOUR PERSONALITY.

A social media account is a great way for viewers to get to know you other than the two minutes you're on the air. Put your best foot forward but be careful about posts that might identify your home address, car license plate, or any other identifiable personal information. If you go on vacation, you might want to wait until you are back home before sharing. You never know. There might be someone out there who will take advantage of you being out of town and rip off your home. Use common sense and be careful.

WHAT I WISH I'D DONE

One of the biggest regrets I have when looking back on my career is that I didn't take any notes about the thousands of stories and people I met over almost forty years in the business. There were so many great stories and wonderful people that I've simply forgotten about.

But thanks to new technology, you don't have to have those same regrets. You carry a high-quality camera with you everywhere you go in your cell phone! I would encourage you to start an account (maybe on Instagram) where every single day you take a picture, or three, of the people you interview and the places you go. Then write a brief description of what you did, who you met, and what you learned. Imagine looking back on that account ten, twenty years down the road. It would be so rich and informative, and I know you would not regret having that record of all that you did. You may not think it's important now, but believe me, you will! So please do me a favor and start that account, even if it's not public and just for you.

ETHICS AND ATTRIBUTION

THERE ARE ENTIRE COLLEGE COURSES AND BOOKS written on the subject of media ethics. There is no way I can cover that much ground in one short chapter. I can, however, lay down some basics to get you thinking with some examples of the challenges you might face and some overriding principles to guide you.

So many times, reporters and MMJs are "out on an island" the entire day faced with having to make decisions about how we approach our stories and maintain fairness and transparency. Hopefully, your station will have some guidelines you can reference, or better yet, a competent manager you can call with any questions.

Even if you do your job perfectly, you'll still get complaints. Sometimes, I've found what's fair to us will not be fair to someone who has a stake in the game (a bias). And sometimes you'll just blow it. You'll forget to ask a key question, you'll be unaware of another side, you'll be tired, hungover, not on your A-game, and you'll make mistakes. That's okay. We're human. But if every time you do a story you ask yourself, "Am I being fair? What would the other side say? How can I address those concerns?" you will be on the right track. It has to be automatic. Ask those questions of yourself *every time.*

And pay attention when your journalistic conscience starts poking you in the side. If you make a mistake, or more accurately, *when* you make a mistake, correct it. Work with your managers to figure out the best way if the story has already aired.

TRANSPARANCY

One way to make sure you maintain integrity in what you do, is to never deceive the audience about how you gathered information for your story. If you're doing a story on traffic at rush hour but you shot your story at noon, be sure and mention that.

> *"We didn't see any traffic backups at noon,*
> *but we'll be back at rush hour to check then."*

If you're using video supplied to you by the company you're doing a story on, include that information.

> *"The company gave us this video to use for*
> *our story, and you can see..."*

You'll probably want to add a caption throughout the use of that video that mentions where it came from. If a viewer provided the video, don't pass it off as your own. There are many reporters involved in "investigations," but don't deceive people, including those you are trying to expose. If you're calling an airline to see what their policy is on lost baggage, you don't necessarily have to identify yourself as a reporter, but if they ask, I think you should be honest and tell them.

Play it straight. Don't use other people's work as your own. Show both sides. Find and report facts. Keep your opinion out of it, but do share what you see, hear, smell, etc. Transparency is just letting viewers see how you got the information you're using for your story. Don't be sneaky; be open with your news gathering process.

Also be careful about secretly recording people in interviews. Generally, if you hold a microphone to their face, they can't claim you secretly recorded them. But there may be times during some stories, especially investigations, where secretly recording someone is necessary. In those cases, make sure your news director is on board with the plan. Generally, audio is the biggest hazard, not video. States have what's known as one- or two-party consent laws. That means you can't record unless either one person agrees to the recording, or in some states, both parties or all parties have to agree. One-party states are easy because as long as you agree, then you're okay to record. But in two-party states both parties have to be informed of the recording. However, it's not that simple because the FCC has its own rules governing secret recordings, and of this writing, they do not allow stations to broadcast one-party consented recordings. Do your homework; talk to your bosses ahead of time. Transparency is always the safe bet.

ATTRIBUTION

One of the most fundamental tools we journalists use to be transparent, fair, and accurate is the concept of attribution. Many of you know what this means and how important this is. But this section is for those who don't. Attribution means you're telling us where you got the information...specifically, who told you. It's absolutely crucial to attribute information and opinions you collect while you are on your story. So that the audience is clear, it's not you who is saying the zoo is mistreating animals, it's the state agency responsible for monitoring the zoo and specifically it's State Inspector Bill Callahan who wrote these exact words in his report.

It's your job to tell viewers what Mary Jones from the zoo told you and to use her exact quote when she says the state is wrong. You tell viewers what the key players are saying and use their exact names every time. Attributing information, facts, accounts, and opinions to others somewhat insulates you from lawsuits and helps protect you in case some of the information later turns out to be inaccurate.

You might find yourself saying to viewers, "The zoo told me last week they didn't have any health problems among the zebras, but today they changed their story and said there were two zebras who'd been taken to Cleveland because they were sick." Contentious or inside information needs attribution the most. You don't have to attribute the fact that the nearby microchip plant smells awful if you're standing there sniffing the air, but you do have to attribute why and tell viewers who besides you is complaining about it.

If you're using an unnamed source, say as much, and also explain why you granted them anonymity. Tell viewers if they have an ax to grind and let them make their own judgments once they know the complete picture. When you have to hide the identities of the people you interview, do so with the permission of the station's management and only for a very good reason like fearing for the safety of an eyewitness or an employer.

In whistle-blower cases, be very sure that what this person is telling you is factual; you need evidence and the accounts of others who work there. Even then, accusing a company of serious misdeeds is dangerous from both an ethical and legal perspective. What are the motives of the person who is talking to you? Do they want to expose injustice, or get even? Remember, attribution doesn't completely prevent you from being sued. If you broadcast unfounded allegations against a company that causes them financial losses, they can go after you and your station in court. And to be honest, just the station having to hire a lawyer can easily surpass your yearly salary in a matter of days.

When you begin working in a new city, it's also very important to know your rights when it comes to interviewing, especially children, and where and when you can do that. Also you need to know where you can go or be restricted from going while doing your job. Generally, journalists have the same rights as the public regarding where they can go and where they can shoot video. Sometimes we have *more* rights.

When I worked in California, California Penal Code 409.5(d) specifically allowed journalists to go past police and fire roadblocks in cases of natural disasters such as mudslides, fires, and earthquakes. The law basically allowed us to enter these dangerous areas at our own risk and report on conditions beyond where the public could go, so long as we didn't interfere with first responders. But that's not the case in many other states. So it's important to know local law.

Even when the law is on your side, that doesn't mean that every firefighter or police officer knows about your rights. Their first instinct is to keep everyone back. The best you can do in these cases is ask for their supervisor and keep going up the chain of command until you find someone who is used to dealing with the media and can help. You don't want to argue and cause a big scene with the frontline folks because you will risk being arrested. There are few stories that are worth pushing things to this level.

If you're on a public street or sidewalk, you have a right to video anything you see. There might be some limitations on using your zoom lens, but in most cases you're legally allowed to shoot what any average person could see. Again, just because you're legally in the right doesn't always protect you from irate homeowners who will yell at you to get out of their neighborhood. Whether you're in the right or not, your safety is always most important. When we knew the story we were on might elicit anger, the plan was always to shoot fast and get out of there quickly. Look for trouble, and most times you'll find it.

What about interviewing children? So far, I've personally never worked in a city where it was against the law to interview or shoot video of children, even without their parents' consent.

But some stations have enacted policies that forbid crews from doing so. Honestly, I think that's a good thing. I wouldn't want reporters interviewing my young children without my permission. Also consider the fact that children you interview could be in hiding from abusive parents. I wouldn't want to be the person who outed them on television. My advice is it's always best to get the parent's permission to interview children under fourteen. And if you shoot large groups of children at the mall or in schools without permission, shoot it in such a way to avoid showing faces, or blur the faces later in editing.

Malls are semipublic places but privately owned. So, yes, the public is allowed there and sometimes folks shoot pictures and videos on their cell phones. But try dragging a big TV camera in there, and you'll see how fast you are told to leave. Malls were always a place I tried to avoid going. If a big story breaks inside a mall, I'd suggest using your cell phone to shoot it instead of attracting attention with a news camera.

Schools are the opposite, they are publicly owned, but access is tightly controlled. You can shoot any school or playground from the sidewalk, but that will probably cause some concern from school employees. It wouldn't hurt to at least give the school or media liaison a call and let them know that you'll be shooting some video of the school. If in doubt, talk with other reporters on staff or your managers to find out how best to handle these delicate shoots.

Just realize how much the appearance of a news camera can cause people's blood pressures to rise. It's best to work with the venue, and be up front, but there will be times when you'll need to get video of places where they don't want you there. Just have a plan, and if you think it's going to be dicey, make sure the station has someone go with you.

OFF THE RECORD

We talked about this a bit before in this book but let's review and add in a few other details. If you've watched any movies about reporters, you've probably heard the term "off the record" before. What does it mean? I'd like to tell you but there really is no standard definition and that's the exact reason why that term can get you into trouble if you're not careful. "Off the record" may mean something totally different to the person feeding you information than it does to you or your boss.

Generally, off-the-record situations come up in one of two ways. The first is when someone calls you and says they have some juicy information about something, but you can't use their name. The second is when it was your idea to interview someone, but the person who has key information for your story refuses to speak for fear of retaliation (or other reasons).

In that second case, it's generally a good idea to ask your manager if it's okay to offer an off-the-record conversation.

There are valid reasons for and against doing so. If you have hard evidence against the mayor that he has been taking bribes, he might offer to talk with you off the record. But what is there to gain? He basically wants to tell his side without being married to the "facts" he's about to spill. Or maybe an aide to the mayor has additional evidence they want to share without being associated with the story. You might offer that person an off-the-record deal to tell you what they know. In this case, you know who the source is and the information provided to you may ignite other angles of investigations you can pursue.

You rarely ever want to take off the record comments and use them verbatim in your story. Rather, the information should be used as a road map for other avenues where you can then use official records or on-the-record quotes, which then become facts in your story.

For example, you wouldn't want to use the aide's off-the-record comment that the mayor also took a bribe when he worked in another city, but you could use that information to search records or talk with other officials in the other city.

When you agree to an off-the-record conversation, you need to also keep your word and make sure the information you are told doesn't expose your source, then have a conversation about how to use that information in a way that makes them comfortable.

Now, when someone approaches *you* for an off-the-record conversation, you have to be even more careful. First, establish who you are talking to. If it's someone claiming to be from a company that they want to expose, you need to meet with them and actually see their work ID or paycheck or something that ties them to the company. Do your research and, again, use their tips as only a starting place in your investigation. Never rely on any tips from phone calls or social media sites and go on the air with them. Confirm, investigate, and do your own research before airing anything. You can't afford to be wrong.

Sometimes you'll get an email from a parent that says, "Don't use my name, but yesterday a child brought a gun to Belmont Middle School." In a case like this, I would definitely honor the request not to use the source's name and my next call would be to the school.

I'd say, "A parent emailed us about a gun found at the school yesterday. What can you tell us about that?" We've had cases where someone new on the assignment desk would acciden- tally forward the parent's email to the school's media person, including the parent's name and email address, when asking for more information. So don't make that mistake. And never report information that is emailed to you without getting con- firmation from an official. Tips sent to you via email or phone calls are often wrong and are often provided by people who heard the information second- or third-hand.

For more on the topic of attribution, I highly recommend taking a look at the Code of Ethics put together by the Society of Pro- fessional Journalists at spj.org.

PAYOLA AND FAVORS

As a reporter, MMJ, or anchor, you're going to come into contact with people who want to give you things. Be extremely careful about accepting them. Your station should have a policy regarding what you can or can't accept. Find out what it is and use your best judgment. In my opinion, it is okay to accept free donuts from a viewer or business if you're out on location at 6:00 a.m. doing fifteen live shots in the snow. It would not be okay to accept a free TV from a company you're doing a story on, however. Be careful about what you accept, especially if it is offered by an entity you're doing a story on. In most cases, it's probably best to politely decline.

On top of getting in trouble with your station, you could get in serious trouble with the FCC if you accept favors, cash, or goods in return for positive treatment of some business or politician. The front-row concert tickets aren't worth risking your job or your reputation. Play it straight.

TELL THE TRUTH

This may seem obvious, but if you just tell the truth, seek the truth, and accept the truth, even when you might not want to, you will have few ethical problems. That means reaffirming what I told you earlier in the book. When you cover a story don't report the story you *thought* you'd see. Report the story you find. The assignment desk, producers, your managers will all have preconceived ideas on what your story is all about, what angle to take, etc. But you are the one who is actually going out into the field. Don't ever be afraid to tell them that what you thought was the story really isn't. Once you make that tough call, your day will go smoother, and you'll go home with a clean conscience.

NIELSEN AND OTHER RATING SERVICES

Don't ever fill out an audience survey from one of the ratings services, such as Nielsen, if you work for a station. Don't influence your friends and be up front and ask your station manager if you have any questions about any other relatives who may have received a survey or been asked to participate in a research study. Simple. Let's move on.

NEWSROOM POLITICS

THIS CHAPTER IS DEVOTED TO helping you get along and thrive in your newsroom. I will tell you a bit about the chain of command, the expectations from your bosses, and the best ways to work alongside your fellow employees. I see over and over again how some people in this business become their own worst enemy in terms of success. So let's begin by discussing the people you'll encounter, what they do, and more importantly what they want from you.

GENERAL MANAGER

This is the big boss of the station who is in charge of everyone who works there. Sometimes a GM will work in the building, but in larger corporations, a general manager may be responsible for several stations in the region, and you might not see them very often. The GM's job is to make sure the station is making money for the company that owns the station. That means the GM monitors whether the sales department is selling as many commercials as possible for the highest rate. The GM is also concerned about ratings because they determine the prices the sales department can charge for those ads and how popular your station will be among advertisers.

The GM has the final say on how to deal with big problems. They are often the cheerleader who will try to build good morale among the sales and news teams. The GM will often hold meetings to keep you aware of station happenings and how your corporate owner is doing and what changes they are making. They are also responsible for budgets, meaning they hold the reins on all the different departments, and they are the ones who have to justify how much money the station needs from the heads of the corporation.

A good GM will be constantly thinking of new ways to make money. Whether that is a new show to add to the schedule, maybe some web feature on a new advertiser, or something the news department can help with, such as a Friday night football show they can sell.

You won't have much contact with the GM. They usually work in a different part of the station than you and probably on a different shift. However, depending on the station, the GM may have the final say on whether you get the job or lose your job (in larger stations, that decision is made by the news director). A GM will want to know that you are competent, have a desire to work hard, that you will honor your contract, and that you're a team player. Just know that the GM holds the most power at any station, and you don't want to alienate that person. Treat them with respect, and I would say give them a wide berth.

NEWS DIRECTOR

It's a general rule of thumb that the smaller the station, the more contact you'll have with the news director. In big markets, the news director's office might be on a completely different floor, and you might rarely see that person unless there's huge breaking news, big trouble, layoff announcements, or to congratulate the staff on winning a bunch of awards.

In really big markets, news directors have assistants who handle the more routine, day-to-day obligations while they focus on the big picture: handling temperamental anchors, working with the GM to improve ratings, and the big one, budgets (finding out how much money the news department needs from corporate and how to make do with the money the company actually coughs up).

In these larger markets, you just want to fly under the radar. Minimal contact is okay. They're busy. You'll want any contact you have with the news director to be positive. What these large-market leaders want from you is not to cause them trouble. Don't get sued, don't get in any car accidents, don't lose your gear, don't get in fights with coworkers.

In small markets, you might wind up working alongside the news director because they don't have the luxury of a big staff or assistants. They will have to get their hands dirty writing scripts, assigning crews, and filling holes in the staff. Smaller markets are actually great for you to get to know your boss on a closer level. These small- to medium-size-market news directors want reporters and MMJs who work hard, have great attitudes, and come up with solutions when they present problems. They don't want to have to babysit you, but they want you to keep them informed when you run across a problem or scenario that could have some kind of backlash on the station. Do your job well, don't be a distraction, have a good attitude, and you'll go far with these managers.

ASSISTANT NEWS DIRECTOR

This may be the manager you'll wind up having the most interaction with. For the sake of simplicity, let's assume the rest of these job titles are in smaller- to medium-size markets. In these markets, the assistant news director is one of the hardest working people in the building. When I did this job, it was really difficult for me to keep track of all the different expectations. There were schedules and editorial decisions, and I had to help implement directives that came from the general manager, passed through the news director, and landed on my desk. I was charged with keeping track of our on-air content, plus I had to manage the concerns, egos, and occasionally the breakdowns of other managers, reporters, anchors, and producers. I had to approve all the reporter scripts and make changes. My favorite part of the job was helping the reporters, MMJs, and anchors get better at their jobs, but just when I had it all figured out, two people would call in sick and I'd have to spend the next two hours trying to beg someone to come in to replace them or do the work myself.

As an assistant news director, what I wanted from MMJs and reporters was for them to come to work armed with a positive attitude and ideas or some plan for where to begin to tackle their stories. I wanted them to care about the stories they were covering and to make them their own. I wanted them to not make errors in their scripts and to be fair and accurate. The fewer problems you can make for this very busy manager, the more you'll be respected and trusted with more responsibility. But as with all these management positions, I also wanted to be informed when there was a problem brewing. The last thing I wanted was for my news director to come to me and say, "Did you know about this?" and not have a clue. Don't be afraid to let your managers know when there is a problem that might wind up on their desk. If you can warn the station with the whole story, it makes it easier to defend you against those who want your head on a platter.

EXECUTIVE PRODUCER

The executive producers work closely with the producers of each newscast. Their main focus is the two or three hours of news they supervise. They want the shows to look as good as they can as far as writing, story placement, graphics treatment, pacing, timing, etc. They help the producers manage all the people working on the newscast including technical staff, assignment desk, anchors, reporters/MMJs, and editors.

During normal working hours, if there's a big management decision to be made, generally the news director or assistant news director will be in the building to help. But in the early-morning or late-evening hours, the executive producer will be the only person there to make those decisions.

What executive producers want from you is someone who turns in a good story on time and communicates well throughout the day about how it's going. They need to know if you need any special graphics or have any concerns about the story you're covering. They want you to be pleasant when they call you in the field to ask questions about your story, and they don't want you to yell at them if they have to move you to a different story at the last minute.

Executive producers can be very pleasant people, or they can be very strict and abrasive. I've had both, and you need to know how to deal with either scenario. Even if they are not your direct supervisor, they work very closely every day with the top managers in the news department. If you alienate them, or are rude to them, the news director will hear about it.

PRODUCER

Producers work very hard, usually tasked with putting together one hour of news per day. That hour is usually the last hour of the day they work. So their seven- or eight-hour workday is all for one show. I like to call producers the architect of the newscast. They decide what stories are in the newscast, where those stories go, how long those stories should be, and they generally write all those stories (unless you work in a large market that has writers).

Have you ever had to write a five-minute speech? Remember how long that feels? Well imagine writing an hour of mini speeches every single day. What makes their job stressful is that they are balancing two strong forces each day. They have to be in control of the entire show, down to the second, yet there are many aspects they have *no* control over.

Almost every day, something goes wrong. A story doesn't get fed in from the network in time to use. An anchor drones on, and good stories that they worked on have to be dropped. Sometimes, reporters miss their slot, which is horrible because that's two or three minutes of content the producer was counting on, teasing, and building up that just vanishes at the last second.

So what producers want is for you to make your slot. Honestly, most of the producers I've worked with aren't so concerned about how good your story looks, just so long as it's there. They're generally too busy to even watch. So that's why it's so important to communicate with producers and let them know if there's any chance at all that your story won't be there in time. And you need to do everything you can to make sure you don't let them down. Even if you have to simplify your story and get up there and toss to a soundbite, that's better than being a no-show in their newscast.

Producers want to be able to trust you not to mess up the show that they've worked so hard on. And they want you to take their direction. If they tell you to wrap it up, even if you had so much more you wanted to say, remember, they have their eyes on the whole show. Your efforts are just one small part of that. So trust them. If they call you in the middle of your day and ask you how to tease your story, don't get angry they interrupted you. Take it as a good thing that they want to be accurate.

ASSIGNMENT DESK

The assignment desk's job in most newsrooms is to create as much worthwhile content as possible each day for the station. I've found over my long career that managers and workers on the desk can be more concerned with quantity rather than quality. They can be oblivious to time, distance, and other factors that limit how many places you can go in a day. That's because their bosses often judge them by the number of stories they can conjure up from their field crews. And heaven forbid they miss a good story that winds up airing on the competition.

Being on the assignment desk is a tough job. I did it for a while on the weekends in Fresno when I was also the newscast anchor. I went as far as buying a portable police scanner so I could take it everywhere with me at work, including the bathroom, just to make sure I wouldn't miss anything. Because if I did miss an important story, there was no one else to blame.

I remember on those very slow weekend days, holding my breath watching the ABC affiliate start their newscast thirty minutes before ours, hoping we didn't miss anything big. Most times we didn't, but the job wasn't good for my sanity. So I have a great deal of empathy for the pressures facing assignment desk workers. They have producers, executive producers, and sometimes upper management breathing down their necks. Hardly ever do they get credit when they find something exclusive, but they sure get blamed when the competition leads with a story they missed.

Keep in mind that what the assignment desk is trying to accomplish sometimes works against your goals. You naturally want to do a good, quality story. But sometimes, they see it as better to have you do a couple of okay stories just to make sure they cover everything. So you have to do a good job of explaining what they will be missing when they call to move you to another story. You need to maintain your cool, treat them with respect, and imagine everything you say will be repeated to a manager because it might. Just explain how long it will really take to pack up and move completely across town, or the fact that if you move now, they'll lose your current story. Once faced with the reality of the situation, most assignment desk staffers will be reasonable and find someone else to move to that story. By the same token, if you can accomplish what they are asking, do it. They'll remember your cooperation and great attitude.

EDITOR

Editors are the unsung heroes at many stations. They are constantly under the gun, face multiple deadlines per day, and are often left to clean up the mess created by others. Their job is to edit many mundane stories from feed material, check those stories off the list, and move on to the next. What editors want in a normal day is to not be stressed, maybe get a chance to show some creativity, and turn out at least one good story.

What they want from you is not to stress them out or feed your material to them late. Give them as much time to edit your story as possible. Talk to them. Tell them if you have ideas. I used to give them a hyped-up description. "Hey, I got some great shots in there for you to use. I'm envisioning kind of a fast-paced story with quick cuts, so I've given you extra time to edit."

Sit in with them if possible. When I was an intern in San Diego, it was really fun to watch the editor, reporter, and the photographer all crammed into the small edit bay, each sharing their ideas of what shot to add next. I know I'm dating myself, but there was really no substitute to being in the room as the story was being edited to really make sure it came out the way it was envisioned. Remember, the editor is starting cold on a story you've worked on all day. It's tough for them to catch up, even if you leave them notes. Be very nice to editors. They can truly make or break your piece, depending on their attitude. Make sure they'll want to do a good job for you.

STUDIO CREW/NEWSCAST DIRECTOR

These professionals are being asked to do more and more and more. Directors at many stations in the country are responsible for up to three, four, maybe even five newscasts a day! And long gone are the days of floor directors, audio technicians, camera operators, graphics operators, and technical directors. Now the directors have to do *everything*, and it's crazy how good the shows look. So just realize many of the directors and any remaining studio crew you'll come into contact with are probably tired and burned out. They need your support and encouragement.

What the studio crew/director wants from you is for you to be ready at least ten minutes before your live shot and to have your package in well before it airs. When you're late, they can't make sure your audio is adjusted, your shot is framed and shaded as it should be, or your IFB is working so you can hear the producer and anchors.

Every newsroom I've ever worked in will distribute a note every six months or so pleading with anchors and reporters not to get to the set, or their live shot, at the last minute. News directors usually ask for fifteen minutes, but ten minutes is usually a fantastic surprise for your newscast directors. Don't make their already tough job harder than it has to be. Be prepared and ready to go well before your shot hits. If you're an anchor, please get to the set at least ten minutes before the show starts.

ENGINEER

You probably won't have too much contact with station engineers, but boy when you need them, you really need them. Engineers have a reputation (along with editors) for being grumpy. I'm not sure why that is. Probably because people are always asking them for something. In fact, I'm sure that's the reason. Just know, like everyone you work with, engineers are asked to do more than ever before, handling all the operating systems in the station, and fixing them when they break down. That means your phone, computer network, and technical systems that get your signal to the transmitter tower and on the air are all their responsibility. And now they even have to troubleshoot air conditioner or heater issues.

When you think of all the different equipment that can break at the station, you'll begin to understand their workload. Again, treat these people with kindness. Say hi to them, especially when you don't need anything from them. Treat them like human beings. Get to know their names. If you can establish a bit of a personal relationship with them, they may begin to see you as more than their next problem or work order.

They want your respect and patience when they can't fix your problem right away. Give that to them freely.

PHOTOGRAPHER

If you are lucky enough to be able to work with a photographer, you'll realize they are your key to happiness at the station. You'll spend more time (at least eight hours) with the photographers than anyone else, including your significant other, crammed into a car or experiencing very intense situations.

A good photographer can make the day go by faster. They can make your story sing, and they can be a person you bounce ideas off of, who will pump you up when you're afraid, and console you when you're down. *And* they can show you the best lunch and coffee spots. Of all the people I've worked with, I can absolutely say my best friends at every station where I was a reporter were members of the photography staff.

After being at a station for a while, you'll discover the shooters who you get along with the best, and you'll develop a rapport with them where you'll know what they're thinking and vice versa. When you get into the zone with that special photog, your stories will be better, and your comfort and confidence will go through the roof.

Photographers want your respect and to be treated as an equal in the story process because they are indeed your equal. Some of the best ideas about how to complete stories came from the photographer I was working with. Give them time and freedom to do their job without micromanaging them. I would never tell a photographer how to shoot something, but I would say, "I would like to use a line in the package that talks about the fall leaves and fall sports. Can you make something work with the kids playing football by those trees?" And they would invariably find a way to make that connection. And many times they'd do it better than the way I was thinking. So trust them, talk to them, bounce ideas off them, and challenge them to create something special every time you go out. And carry their tripod!

Now that we've gone through the major newsroom roles, I want to share what helped me rise through the ranks and be successful at a number of stations. So back by popular demand: Wayne's Top Ten, this time for excelling at newsroom politics.

1. DON'T GOSSIP.

I know this is a tough ask in a newsroom, but try to stay above the pettiness and gossip that takes place. It's okay to know who's dating who, but don't engage in the negative gossip where people put others down. You'll be so much more respected if you use your time to raise people up; support, help, and collaborate with other reporters/MMJs. Positivity and cheering for others definitely gets noticed. It gets you quick friends and loyalty as well. If, on the other hand, you try to raise yourself up by putting others down, people will remember that, too, even if they seem like they are agreeing with you at the time.

2. DON'T SAY THE FIRST THING YOU FEEL WHEN YOU'RE ANGRY OR FRUSTRATED.

There will be many, many times when a manager or coworker will call or text you and ask you to do something you don't want to do. My friends and I called it the "Hey, buddy" call. "Hey, buddy, can you ____?"

> *"Hey, can you please drive by this location on your way back to the station?"*

> *"Hey. John called in sick. Can you possibly work tomorrow?"*

> *"Hey, buddy, how far along are you on your story because we may need to move you to breaking."*

Your first impulse (like mine was) might be to say, "No! I can't do that! Do you have any idea how hard we've been working to get this story?"

But then after you hang up, you start to feel bad, and you start to actually process the request. Then you realize (most of the time) that you could have probably done what they were asking. So in these situations I'm suggesting you take a deep breath and tell them you'll call them right back. Take two minutes to really think about it. If you can't do what they are asking, you'll be much calmer after a couple of minutes and you'll be able to give them legitimate reasons why. If you can do it, then you can own it and display a positive attitude. Let me explain what I mean by "owning it."

If you're going to have to do something you really don't want to do anyway, it's much better to be positive about it. It happens all the time in relationships. My wife will say, "Honey, can you take out the garbage?" as she's working hard to clean the house. I know I'll need to do it eventually. So I can either say, "No! Can't you see I'm watching football?" And then I'll feel bad and go do it anyway in a huff, and she'll be angry. Or I could stop and think for a couple of minutes, wait for a commercial, then say, "Of course I can take out the garbage. It's the least I can do. And by the way, what else do you need help with?" This way, she feels better about asking me, I feel better about doing it, and everyone wins. So next time the assignment desk calls you and asks if you can go somewhere, give it some real thought, and if you're going to do it, own it. Say, "Sure I can do it! I'm on my way!" rather than, "I don't want to do it, but if you're going to make me, fine."

3. BE CAREFUL WITH ROMANTIC RELATIONSHIPS WITH PEOPLE AT WORK.

I know it happens all the time. It's only natural that there will be some romantic entanglements going on when you spend so much time with other attractive, mostly single, similar-minded people. Just know that some of these relationships won't work out, and you'll still have to work with them even if it goes bad. And if you do pursue a romantic relationship with a coworker, keep it professional at work. No one wants to see you guys making out in the parking lot or in a back room.

4. BE SOMEONE YOUR MANAGER WANTS TO SEE WALKING INTO THEIR OFFICE.

I'm sure someone else thought of this before I did, but it's a technique I've used for a long time that really seems to work for building good relationships with my bosses. Try to make contact with them when things are going well. Pass on just a bit of good news to them with a smile every time you make an effort to see them. Maybe your station just won an Emmy, maybe their favorite team won a ball game, maybe you just got a great interview the day before. The goal is to consistently take literally one minute or less, to peek your head into their office and give them some good news. *Then get out of there.* Then they start **associating you with good things**. It works.

Look at the other side of the coin. I had people come into my office all the time, and before they even said a word I knew it was going to be bad news and a difficult conversation. YOU DO NOT WANT TO BE THAT PERSON! If you are constantly complaining, your bosses will associate you with negativity and maybe think of you as a negative person. I hate to break this to you, but if that's how you act, maybe that is indeed what you are.

But if you bring positive vibes to the office, not only will your boss start associating you with positivity, but on those rare occasions that you do have a problem, they will take you more seriously. They'll think, *Hey, here's a person who never complains. If they are complaining now, it must be important.*

5. COMMUNICATE.

I've brought this up a lot for good reason. Let people know when there is a problem that might affect the newscast or the station. Let them know what's happening in the field. They won't know if you don't tell them.

6. DON'T YELL.

No one likes a screamer. If absolutely necessary, do it outside or in your car. Don't yell at your coworkers for any reason. It's not respectful or professional and has no place at work.

7. BE PREPARED.

Have a go-bag ready to go in case you need to cover a story in another state. Be ready for the unexpected. If you have the capacity to be the person they can count on, do so.

8. VOLUNTEER.

There's no better way to stand out than standing up when no one else is willing. Again, own it! If no one wants to do a story and you can, speak up. "I'd like to try to tackle that story." Meet the challenge. Take some risks. Go the extra mile when possible. In the end, you'll find what really wasn't so hard or took you that long will build you much more goodwill with your bosses that you can cash in when you really need it. Maybe you want three weeks to go to Europe on vacation. They will remember all you did for the station and take that into account when considering your request.

I hope this doesn't come off as sounding too transactional. But in some ways, that's exactly what it is. (Remember when I said I'd be honest?) I've found that in most any job, you get out what you put in. At least, that's the way it should be. If your bosses don't take care of you when you take care of them, then maybe you need a better place to work.

9. BE A GOOD CITIZEN.

Don't be a jerk at work or in public. Treat people with respect. Get involved with your community. Be nice to people you meet in restaurants, coffee shops, and tire stores. Live up to your good image. Show up on time. Don't be late. Don't cut out early unless someone says it's okay. Don't ever, ever lie on a timecard. Don't ever drive a station vehicle after you've been drinking. Take care of your gear. Treat it like your own.

10. WHEN YOU COME WITH A PROBLEM, BRING A SOLUTION.

Everyone has problems—your story, someone you work with, your hours, etc. When I was a manager, I would appreciate an employee who would come to me with possible solutions to their problems. I could tell that they thought about it and weren't just coming to complain. This is so important. Don't just say, "That can't be done." Say, "I can't do that because of this, but here's what we can do!" It makes a huge difference.

HOW DO YOU KNOW HOW YOU'RE DOING?

I've learned over the years that some people have a hard time seeing the signs when they might be on the outs with their station. Or, conversely, if they are really admired.

If you are doing well at a station as a reporter or MMJ, you'll receive compliments about your stories, your live shots, or your attitude. Managers will assign you the hardest, most important stories. They will count on you to turn stories under tight deadlines. You will be among the first to be sent out of town for an overnight trip. You're not being picked on; it's the opposite. You've earned their trust. And chances are, you'll be the lead reporter in the newscast more often than not. Be glad. You worked hard for this. And when your contract is up, management will do their best to keep you. But you might be ready to move to a larger market, and if your managers are honorable people they'll most certainly give you a great recommendation.

Now let's look at the flip side. How will you know if you are not highly thought of at work or possibly about to be fired? Chances are, you'll get all the easy stories. You won't lead many newscasts. Managers may be short with or apathetic to you. Your job reviews probably won't be great. You'll probably be called into the boss' office once or twice and hear words like "attitude," "missing," "late," and "errors." You won't be getting along with other members of management or staff. Try to avoid being in this position (you won't be if you take my advice in the rest of this book).

Additionally, you'll know you are on your last strike when you get a written warning that you have to sign. That usually means you are one step away from being fired. Even then, you have time to turn it around, but you have to want it. If you really hate your job and the people you work with, you should really plan your escape and try to leave. Life is too short to be miserable. Sometimes, for whatever reason, good people don't succeed at one station but do very well at the next. Maybe it just wasn't a good fit.

Just as there are bad employees out there, there are also bad managers. If you are stuck with one (or two) of them, life can be hell for you. I've had some managers at some number-three stations I've worked for change their goals, news philosophies, and story judgment overnight. They were so busy chasing the top stations in the market, they'd pull reporters off a great story just so we could do the same stories another station did. So, they'd not only ruin the story we were working on, but because the other station had a seven-hour head start on us, our copy-cat story would be lousy.

Station management, position in the market, and ownership should all be very important to you when seeking a job in the first place. Do your research before signing a contract.

HOW TO LAND A JOB OR MOVE UP

IN THIS CHAPTER, we'll go over your reel, résumé, agents (whether you should get one), recruiters, talent placement agencies, and contracts. We'll address a bit about interviewing for a job as well as your social media pages and even your voicemail. I will give you my most honest advice and I want you to know I have no dog in the fight. I'm not beholden to anyone about what I write here. I'm simply someone who has been able to get some great jobs and also been on the other side of the desk interviewing reporter, MMJ, and anchor candidates.

Let's start with those of you who are presently in, or just out of college. You probably have a million questions. I want to begin by saying most colleges excel at getting students prepared for the real world. I'm sure you've already had way more experience handling a camera and putting a story together than I did at your age. On top of that, the job market as I write this is heavily tilted in your favor. Stations simply cannot find enough capable candidates to fill all their open positions. That's great news for you.

When I was looking for a reporting job in 1986, news directors had stacks and stacks of tapes on the shelves of their offices. I was competing against many other talented people and just hoping for the rare opening. There was no social media or YouTube then. I had to physically make an audition tape, on professional equipment, and then mail that tape to the news directors in markets where I thought I had a chance at finding a job. It wasn't cheap to buy the tapes, pay the postage, or find a place to edit, especially for a starving college student who didn't know where his next beer was coming from.

Now you can simply edit your reel on your laptop, post it to YouTube, and email a link to whomever you want. You can post your work on a number of websites and get yourself noticed. There are a number of people who will be happy to assist you in getting that first or next job. So, let's go over how I would go about getting a job if I were graduating college today.

NARROW YOUR SEARCH (START WITH THREE CITIES)

You are in a great position as there are way more jobs than applicants. So narrow down the cities where you want to work. Consider lifestyle, cost of living, and market size. You want to pick a small- to medium-size market where you have a good chance of landing a job. Concentrate on three cities, then do your research on those cities and rank them in order of preference.

How much would you need to make to live in those cities? What is the average rent? Which part of these cities would be safest, most exciting, or most convenient in getting to the station? What issues do those cities face? How is crime? Is there enough there for you to do outside of work? What attractions or parks are nearby? How far is it from your hometown? Would you want to go back to your family for holidays, and how much would that cost? Once you compute all of that, start seeking out the right station.

DRILL DOWN ON STATIONS, RATINGS, AND CORPORATE OWNERS

Take a hard, extensive look at the stations that serve that market. Who's ranked number one in the ratings? Who's last? Who owns the stations, and what is the reputation of those companies? What other stations do those companies own? If you really want to someday have a dream job in San Diego, it might be good for you to find a station in a smaller city that is owned by a company that also has a station in San Diego. You'll find it's much easier to move up within a company than it is to be an outsider.

Once you've figured out your top city and your two top stations in that city, reach out to people at those stations, and ask what it's like to work there. Go to the stations' websites and start following all the reporters on social media. Find some staffers who seem approachable and message them. "I just graduated and am thinking about applying at your station. Can you tell me what it's like to work there?" Some people may be reluctant to say anything bad about their station, but some may be very honest with you. If they say they don't want to talk to you about it, that may be a sign to stay away.

On the other hand, if people you contact gush about how great their station is, you should take that to heart and concentrate on that station. I'd be wary, though, of working for the number-three or four-rated station in the market. As a person who's worked for a number-one and number-four station, I can honestly say there is a big difference. A top station is usually stable and has good equipment and managers who've been there for a long time. The station is consistent in their approach in how they cover news. The station in last place has lots of management turnover and is probably constantly changing or reinventing itself to find the right formula to overtake the market leaders. That turmoil makes it tough on the staff.

TAP INTO CORPORATE RECRUITERS AND TALENT PLACEMENT AGENCIES

So far we've talked about going it alone in your job search, but there are many resources out there, and you should absolutely take advantage of that. Let's continue now and include folks who are looking for their *next* job after already being in the business for a while.

There are two excellent resources for you to consider no matter if you're coming out of college or a seasoned vet. Corporate recruiting has really gained ground over the past few years, and I see major broadcasting companies investing more resources into this area. This move toward aggressively searching for job candidates came from the lack of job seekers entering the market. TV station owners have discovered that it is far more beneficial to actively search for job candidates versus waiting for candidates to come to them. So corporate recruiters go to universities, show up at industry conventions, and work the rooms at awards ceremonies trying to feed the hungry machine of TV news operations across the country.

So you need to find out who these recruiters are and do what it takes to get on their list. Make sure they have your current reel, contact information, and résumé. They in turn will put all that information on their internal corporate website that individual news directors can search and pick from. This service is free. Take advantage of it. Get on these lists! But do not sign anything that says you are committing exclusively to them.

Another very similar service involves private companies who work with and for TV stations and corporations to find them talent. Most of these folks have been doing this decades and have deep contacts in many different markets. They do the same service as corporate recruiters and create lists with résumés and reels they can then hand over to their TV station clients. Again, it's either a free service for you or costs a very minimal charge to get on these talent placement lists. These non-TV-owned businesses do a great job reaching stations that don't have their own recruiting departments. Getting on as many of these lists as possible ensures more news directors can see your reel with little to no effort on your part.

AGENTS

Oh, boy, here we go. I know many people will disagree with me, but I'm writing this book for you, not them. My opinion is that there is much less of a reason for you to hire an agent today than ever before. Given how much easier it is to get your reel seen by hundreds of news directors, the need for a personal TV agent is only appropriate for a select group of people in our business.

Agents will charge you between five and twelve percent of your gross salary once they find you a job. Think about how much money that is! If you make $70,000 a year, they take $7,000 off the top if you sign for the standard ten percent. Again, that's off your gross pay, not your net! Over the course of a three-year contract, that's $21,000 dollars you're paying to your agent—the price of a car!

"Yeah, but Wayne, an agent can get me a lot more money than I could have negotiated on my own." Well, that's not true if you're trying to get your first or second job. When you are looking for most MMJ/reporter jobs in non-top-ten markets, news directors will have a very narrow window of how much they can pay you. So I can say with confidence that an agent will not get you significantly more money than you could have negotiated on your own.

They may be able to get you other perks, such as a few more vacation days, or make sure your contract doesn't have any weird clauses that may cause you trouble later, but you can easily pay a lawyer to look over your contract and be way ahead. Plus, more and more companies are going to generic contracts for all of their employees to sign, and they are very hesitant to approve any big changes to that boilerplate language.

So my advice is, if you are just starting out in this business, or even if you are looking for your second job, do not get an agent. While it's true they only start taking your money once you start working at the job they got you, they will be along for the ride for your entire contract with the station, and the separate contract you have with the agent sometimes makes it hard to ever get rid of them, even if you move to a new station three years later.

I think agents still provide a valuable service, but only to people who are very good at their jobs and work for a station or network that has a lot of discretion in how much they pay. So for extremely talented sports announcers who really want to work for ESPN or another network, it might be a good idea to sign with an agent who specializes in that field. They will have great contacts to help get your work seen, they will know of openings before they happen, and they will be in the right position to put your name at the head of the line if they feel you are right for the job. Then, they can negotiate your contract, which could net you much more money than you'd ever get on your own. Primary anchors who work in top ten, even top twenty markets, might want an agent to help negotiate contracts and serve as a go-between to head off any problems with management.

Anyone who really wants to work at the network level could probably benefit from the services of an agent. But be smart about signing a contract with them. Unlike TV stations, agents have more discretion to negotiate with you by lowering their rates and narrowing their contracts to, for instance, only apply if they get you a specific job. If they want you, they'll agree to your demands.

It's also important that if you have a great relationship with the agent who is recruiting you, make sure your agreement specifies that if that agent ever leaves the agency you are free to leave as well.

I am not anti-agent. I had a great agent for most of my career who I believe served me well. But I feel that with the number of jobs available and the shortage of talent, agents are just not needed for the jobs newcomers to the industry will be qualified for.

YOUR REEL, YOUR KEY TO EMPLOYMENT

In most businesses, it's all about the résumé. With TV news, it's all about the reel. What do you look like on TV? That's what it's all about. Just as there are different kinds of people, I believe that every news director is a little bit different in what they are looking for in that reel, but there is some definite common ground in what makes a good reel versus a bad one. So let's discuss how you can put together a reel that will show what you can really do.

In the case of length, I don't think there is a definitive answer for this. My opinion is ten to fifteen minutes is a good length. It's enough time for them to see how you handle different types of stories and to get a feel for your personality. But it's not so long as to bore them. You'd rather leave them wanting more, not hitting the stop button.

The reel you present should be appropriate to the job you are seeking. If you're applying for a reporter job, you should start with some stand-ups or live shots because they want to see *you*! If you are applying for an anchor job, show yourself in the studio anchoring different stories.

When including stand-ups, you want to have a mixture of hard news and feature stories to show how you handle different situations. So I'd say start your reel with about five stand-ups or live shots, then give a full story that you've written to show how you do with story structure, finding focus, and your voice track delivery. Then show another story that might have a lighter or different tone. Then if you do have any anchoring experience, you can include a little of that at the end.

The goal of the reel is to show that you can do the job and are good at it, or at least have potential. I would rather hire someone with a good attitude who's rough around the edges than someone who is very polished but comes across as aloof. I want to see a genuine person on that reel, not someone "being a reporter." I hope that makes sense.

Ask ten people how to assemble a reel and you'll get ten different answers. Any formula will work as long as you include variety—different scenarios—and a clip that highlights who you really are. It's easier now to adjust your reel, which you should be doing often to include your latest work.

When I was trying to get jobs, I always put my best stories on my reel. Then news directors would always write me back and say, "Okay, that's great, but now send me a reel of all the stories you did last week." They not only want to know the best of what you can do, they want to see the quality of what you churn out every day.

RÉSUMÉS AND COVER LETTERS

I've seen hundreds of TV résumés in my life but probably never looked at one for more than two minutes. Where'd you work, where did you go to school, any interests? Okay, got it. The reel is the most important part of your application, so make your résumé simple and functional.

On the other hand, the cover letter is very important because it shows your writing ability. Generally, the cover letter you write should not be more than a page long and really shouldn't be more than about four or five short paragraphs, but it should be your most quality writing. Address the letter to whoever is making the hiring decisions and be absolutely sure of the spelling of the person's name and don't address any certain gender (names are not an indication of gender). You'd be surprised how many times people make the wrong assumptions and blow their chances for an interview. The thinking is, *I'm hiring a reporter who is supposed to be a fact checker and they didn't even know how to spell my name. Forget it.*

When you write your cover letter, show excitement; show you know something about the station and the job. Tell them something about yourself. Then edit and re-edit it. The next day, look at it and shorten it again! Make every single word perfect. Once I wrote such a great letter, I absolutely believe it got me my job in Seattle. I didn't even send a tape. It was a very novel approach, but based on the quality of my letter, they were actually invested and curious about receiving my reel. Great cover letters stand out. Make yours do the same!

THE VALUE OF A STATION VISIT

It's not always affordable or feasible for you to visit a station before you accept a job offer. But if there is any possible way for you to do that, you should, even if you have to pay for it yourself. You can meet the managers face to face, and you might get a leg up on your competition. Figure out what you want and then go get it. Don't be scattered, throwing your attention all over the country. If you really want to work in a city or for a certain station, focus all your energy on that, whether there is a posted opening or not.

I've actually always avoided applying to stations with a job opening because I figured I'd just be one of a dozen folks applying. So I'd apply when there *wasn't* a job opening. That way, if I hit it off with the news director, I'd be among the first they thought of when there was an opening (and there will always be openings). That advice may not work the same way now, but it's an idea to keep in your back pocket. There are way more openings now than ever, which is good for you. Just figure out which station you really want to work for and make sure it lives up to your expectations.

When you visit, try to just sit in the newsroom and listen and observe for a few minutes. What does it *feel* like sitting there? Do you feel relaxed or is tension building inside of you? I think there is a definite good or bad energy associated with newsrooms. In the bad ones, you might hear yelling, people arguing, and you can literally feel the stress and frustration. In good newsrooms, you hear laughing, people helping other people, you see people smiling, someone might come over and introduce themselves to you. These are the places you want to work.

CONTRACTS

Simply put, contracts spell out the basics of your employment agreement with the station. It states how much money you'll make, how much vacation/sick time, and holiday hours you'll accrue, and the really big one, how long you are bound to work at the station.

Contracts are written by the station's lawyers, or more likely by the lawyers working for the corporation that owns the station. They include legal language, clauses, and spell out what you have to do and what you can't do. As I mentioned earlier, unless you are a top anchor, stations will be very resistant to changing any portion of the contract. So in many cases, it's a take-or-leave-it deal. That doesn't mean you can't ask for changes; maybe you'll get lucky. But you do need to be very sure you understand each clause, and accept those you can live with.

If you find a portion of the contract you do not agree with, you should say so. And be ready to turn down the job if they can't change it. Don't sign something you can't live with! Once your name goes on the dotted line, it will be very difficult and expensive to break the contract.

Contracts always favor the station. So it's not unusual at all to see a contract where you can't leave for two or three years, but the stations will have a period of time each year when they can cancel the deal and let you go. If you have some value to the station, like maybe you've already been there for five years, you can ask for a no-cut deal where you're both bound for the full three years. But stations are reluctant to give away that kind of leverage.

As nerve-racking as it is, signing your (life away) first contract, there will be more to come in later years. Usually, in the last month or two of your current deal, your manager will approach you and ask to start negotiations for a new contract. The new contract should always include a raise, though if your company has merit raises, they may not include yearly salary bumps in your next deal. So they should give you a raise for signing the new contract, but may not give you any additional guaranteed money beyond that.

If your current contract is at $55,000 a year, your new contract might be $65,000 per year for three years. Some companies used to say that the longer you were there, the more valuable you were to them, so they'd structure a three-year contract at $65,000 for the first year, $68,000 for the second, and $72,000 for the third. That's not always the case anymore.

My best advice for those of you going through this process is to know your worth and never bluff. Knowing your worth means having a very realistic view of what value you bring to the station. Are you honestly one of the top-two reporters or anchors there? If you are, you may be able to convince your bosses to give you more money.

When I was in Los Angeles, I felt I was one of the better reporters in the city. I'm not bragging, it's just what I felt in my heart. So when it came time to renegotiate, I first learned what other reporters in town were making then asked for a contract that would pay me in that range. It was a pretty significant bump at the time, and they eventually agreed. But I also wouldn't bluff. If you say you need X number of dollars to stay at the station, even if you're willing to take less, know that your bosses can say at any point, "Well, we're not able to pay that. Good luck at your next job." And just like that, you're out. Don't play hardball unless you are really willing to leave. I was at that time, and it worked for me. In another point in my career, I really needed to spend more time with my family, and I asked to work part-time for a while. I was honestly ready to leave if they didn't agree. Thankfully they did. Eventually, I went back full time, and I think it wound up being a good thing for all of us. But I knew my bosses very well, and they knew me. And I had built up a lot of goodwill with them, and the time came to use up some of it.

Always keep your eye on the prize. What is the result you want from any contract? What amount would make you happy? What is the lowest amount you'll accept? You have to know before you negotiate or else you'll never make a deal that is good for you. That's why it's so important to do your homework on what it costs to live in the cities that interest you. A salary of $50,000 may go pretty far in one city, while in another, you might have to get a roommate to afford the rent.

ATTITUDE IN INTERVIEWS

One of the most important aspects of landing your dream job is to come in with a great attitude. You should be genuinely excited about the job, the station, and the city. Then make sure the people interviewing see that excitement. Try to make sure they understand you are hungry to learn and have a thirst for direction and that you are coachable.

So many people in news are beaten down, pessimistic, and burned out. It's not all their fault. This business can be really tough. But that's also why people who are positive, uplifting, and have can-do attitudes stick out and can greatly separate themselves from the rest of the pack. Show them what you can do, how eager you are to get started, and make it impossible for them to pass you over. You are perfect for this job because, after all, you did your research, and they're not only picking you, you're picking them!

Before the job interview, research the major players at the station. Watch some newscasts and write down some memorable positive points about the newscast you can bring up.

> *"That was a great nat sound package your photographer did on that roller coaster."*

> *"I like the way you guys treated weather the other day when you had that alert about possible tornadoes."*

Know who owns the station—what kind of company they are and their priorities. Ask good questions regarding their priorities for you, the position, expectations, etc. Feel free to ask about pay and benefits, time off, etc. If they are inviting you down for a station visit, make sure to talk about pay before you go. You need to know what they'll offer is in the ballpark of what you need to make. No use wasting their or your money traveling there if the salary won't work for you.

GETTING YOUR HOUSE IN ORDER

Before you apply for jobs or contact recruiters, make sure your public persona is professional. They'll be searching your social media accounts, so you might want to make sure there's nothing that would scare away a prospective employer. You'll probably need a list of references, so make sure the people you list have agreed to provide you with a positive recommendation beforehand. Don't leave it to chance.

Listen to your voicemail right now to make sure it sounds professional. Keep it simple and to the point. If you haven't changed your voicemail message since high school or college, you need to update it. Don't use music or any gimmicks and speak clearly. Also make sure the email address you're using doesn't have some strange nickname that may turn off an employer. You may be a fabulous candidate, but if your email is opinionatedfoole@ xxx.com they may have second thoughts about you. If you don't already have one, create a professional email account using your name that you can use for job interviews.

STAYING POSITIVE

I'D LIKE TO TAKE A FEW MOMENTS to address now the toll the news business can take on a journalist and offer some tips and advice on how to deal with it. So many people are leaving the business, I believe, because no one ever fully told them what they were getting into or how to cope with the everyday stress of telling the best, but mostly the worst, of what's happening in their communities.

Some people are leaving the biz because their managers and corporate owners have unrealistic workload expectations (especially from MMJs). I saw a job posting for an MMJ with the description which asked candidates to "develop, research, write, shoot, edit, and produce, two to three stories a day." In my view, that is a big ask, especially if you're demanding that workload day in and day out. That is a recipe for burnout and failure. Just because technology has made it *possible* to do this doesn't mean it's practical.

When I started in this business, cameras were heavy and required a separate unit to be able to record what the camera saw. This meant not only did a reporter have a photographer to help but sometimes an audio person, too. Then along would come an engineer driving a live truck so that your photographer could edit the story and the engineer could tune in a live signal. It was great working with a photographer because you could write, research, and think, while the other half of your news-gathering team would drive. Now MMJs are expected to do all those jobs at once. And because cameras are lighter and laptops can be used to edit and send in stories, we assume we can get the same amount or more work out of one person that we used to get from three workers. No. That's not right. Even if the tools are more advanced, when your workload is so great, MMJs cannot be creative, will make mistakes, and the overall quality will suffer. It's a frustrating situation to be in. It'd be one thing if MMJs got three salaries to do all the jobs, but in most cases, they're making less than a reporter, which is not right. But until someone reinvents the news business, that's what we're left with. That's why it's so important for you to find a great, supportive place to work, even if it's not where you hoped to end up.

Before discussing mental health, I want to make clear that I am not a mental health professional. So, if you are having any signs of depression, anxiety, or even feelings of exhaustion, please see an expert who can really help you. It's nothing to be ashamed of. Most stations have health plans that include mental health. And

I think most everyone in our business realizes how important it is to make sure you are able to process and deal with the traumatic events we are sent to cover.

No matter where you work in news, you will be in a stressful environment. That's a fact of life for a TV journalist. There is always a deadline looming, sometimes multiple deadlines in just one day. But I have a few suggestions to make it easier to get through the day, and eventually through your career.

MARATHON, NOT A SPRINT

There is no way you can go full speed for every story, every day. You will burn yourself out. You need to adopt a calm and measured approach. Walk, don't run. Be smart with your time. Don't get too down when you fail; don't get too excited with your victories. Just enjoy each day that you can go out into the world and find a story to tell.

GET YOUR WORK IN EARLY

Something that will age you the most in this business is the constant daily deadline stress. My philosophy when I was reporting was always to work hardest at the beginning of my day and try to get the story done as quickly as I could. Write early, get it edited. Maybe don't upload it right away, though. Have an iced tea, some juice, or a cup of coffee first.

If you are racing against the clock every single day, it will take a toll on you. Don't waste time early in your day. Work smart, and get your story written. You will have so much less pressure that way, and if something else comes up or your story needs to change, you're in a position to deal with that.

GET IN A COFFEE, GET IN A LUNCH

I think it's also important that you take a coffee break at some point during your day, and also to make time to get a lunch as often as you can during the week. I know there are many days when that seems impossible, but you must really make an effort to work in a break or two. Think of it as important to your mental health and longevity in this business. You need to find ways to cut corners, cut out the unnecessary work and focus only on the meat of your story. Most days, that allows you time for a half-hour break. If you spend your day running from location to location, especially if you're alone, without taking time to eat, you'll be running on fumes, and by the end of the day you won't be able to think. Make the time to give your brain and body a rest.

DON'T TAKE IT PERSONALLY

You have to be able to separate your work life from your personal life. Just as you need a break in your day, you also need a break from thinking about work when you go home. Exercise is a great way to de-stress and take your mind off your day. Be careful about using alcohol or some other drug to do this. It's easy in this business to fall into the trap of trying to numb yourself from your worries. It may work temporarily, but there will be a price to pay if you're not careful. Blow off steam in other ways. Talking to friends and family also helps. Do your best to find ways to release that pressure.

As reporters, we're expected to be unbiased when telling our viewers about the sometimes-tragic events that occur in our cities. But as human beings, it's not always easy to stay disconnected. So maybe we shouldn't. We're not robots. I think that is only natural for a story to affect you in an emotional way.

When I was working in Los Angeles, I got sent to cover the school shooting tragedy at Columbine High School in Colorado. One moment I was watching scenes in the newsroom of high school kids running away from their school. The next I was there, seeing the aftermath firsthand. It was warm when the shooting happened, and people were wearing shorts. When we landed, I remember the temperatures being in the seventies, and it was sunny.

The students we saw on that first day were for the most part composed and fairly calm after such a devastating event. What I didn't know then, but learned later, was that those kids were in shock. They simply hadn't had time to process what had happened. They didn't know, or at least they hadn't yet realized, they'd never see so many of their classmates again.

Over the next few days as we covered the story, the weather changed, and it snowed. I remember my photographer and I had to buy warmer clothes. It also just happened to be my birthday on day three of our shooting coverage. By then, students had realized the full extent of what had happened. I remember walking around the school on my birthday surrounded by small groups of teenagers hugging and bawling. And it hit me what a gigantic loss had occurred right there on that beautiful campus and what a senseless act of cruelty and violence it was. It is a birthday I will never forget. Since that day, every year, I always think about those kids and what they went through.

You may cover a story and think at the time that it had no effect on you, but later it hits you when you least expect it. Just know that when it happens you need to recognize it and take care of yourself.

A CALLING

You've probably heard from a professor, boss, or guest speaker that journalism is a duty, a calling, to serve the community. I agree. Journalism is a noble profession—one of the few specifically addressed by our founding fathers who worked hard to ensure we had protections to do our job. It's that important.

In the U.S. Constitution, we're mentioned right there in the first amendment:

> *Congress shall make no law respecting an establishment of religion, or prohibiting the free exercise thereof; or abridging the freedom of speech, or of the press; or the right of the people peaceably to assemble, and to petition the Government for a redress of grievances.*

I firmly believe without freedom of the press our country would cease to be recognizable. We are the watchdogs of government; we are the mouthpiece of no one but truth. We stand as one of the key pillars of democracy like police, firefighters, doctors, nurses, and teachers who answer their own call to duty.

We also need to be able to pay rent, feed our families, and earn enough money to live a decent life. Never forget your work serves a very important purpose, and you have worth.

FINAL WORD

Like any other occupation, there is no guarantee you'll have a positive experience. So it comes down to how you live your life. If you're generally a positive person, you'll be able to see the good we do—how the light we bring to issues can make a difference in the lives of so many people.

If you are generally pessimistic, working as a reporter certainly won't improve your state of mind. We see the extremes of society and the very worst of humanity, and we tell their stories. To do that properly we have to understand, empathize, and, yes, feel some of what they are trying to tell us, so that we can then convey the whole story to viewers. This job is not for everyone. As a journalist you have to take the good *and* the bad. It's just life. And if you think you'd have a real problem dealing with this negative side, maybe news is not for you. It's fine. There are other areas in the field of communications which you may be better suited.

But it's not all gloom and doom every day. Along with all the heartache, we also see the very best of people. We see those who pour out their hearts, helping their neighbors and others overcoming odds to succeed when no one thought they would. These stories of hope give reason to believe that there still is much goodness out there.

The best we can hope for as journalists is to be true to ourselves and be true to the stories that we are granted the incredible privilege to tell. Most days, you're not changing the world or even a small part of it. But you live for those rare days where your stories can make a difference. Be ready to push your stations to do more of those stories. We need people with integrity who approach their work with a sense of nobility and aren't just trying to promote themselves on TikTok. We need you because there are too many good and important stories out there and not enough of us to tell them.

ANCHOR TAG

I'VE TRIED TO TELL IT TO YOU STRAIGHT in this book. It's the reality as I know it, anyway—my reality. Yours may be different.

This job can be fascinating. It's a job where if you are open to it, you will learn something new every day, taught to you personally by experts in their respective fields.

The people who you speak to will trust you to share their stories in a truthful, honest way. And you'll do it because you care.

The stories you work hard at turning will be seen by thousands of people. On your good days, you'll enlighten those people. On your best days, you'll touch some of those people and cause them to think and maybe even act to make their communities better.

TV journalists are given such a wonderful opportunity every single day. We are the eyes and ears of our community, and they trust us to tell them what they need to know.

This job—this career—has been so good to me. I was driving home the other day from a camping trip on the Oregon Coast, and it was dark and rainy in the middle of the day. It reminded me so much of my time as a reporter in Seattle back in the early 1990s when I'd ride with photographers who were all much older than I was, and much wiser, too. We'd take these long winter trips to flood-prone areas like Carnation, Mount Vernon, and Fir Island, and the rain would be pounding down on the windshield. We'd be dressed in knee- or even hip-high rubber boots and Gore-Tex, and we'd grab lunch at a gas station and be live in four shows.

It was a lot of work, but looking back, it was so great. We were sent on a mission to capture a story. We were given almost no direction except maybe from a (paper) map. The rest of the story was up to us to find, shoot, and bring back for our viewers. I have forgotten way more stories than I remember, but I'll never forget the excitement, nervousness, and feeling of accomplishment that I'd have at the end of a good, or even average, day.

If you stick with this job, you'll get faster and better at telling stories. You'll be able to find your focus quicker. You'll move up to bigger markets where the people who surround you are also better, faster, and work smarter, and that will bring your game up even more.

From my time in Seattle, I went on to become a staff reporter in Los Angeles and worked with some of the best photographers on

Earth. It wasn't just their shooting ability. What left me in awe was their adaptability to turn on a dime and make a story work at the last minute when it seemed impossible. And they did it all so calmly, usually with a laugh and a smile. We had great times navigating L.A. traffic, many days spending twice as much time driving to the story than we did shooting, writing, and editing the story. And every day was different. When you left home for work, you'd never know where the day would take you. I used to joke with friends that I could be anywhere on the planet at the end of my shift. Working in that number-two market, I never knew when I'd be ordered to head to LAX to get on a flight to a big breaking story.

I wouldn't trade my career in news for any other. I met so many people, worked with so many great friends, and then got to share my work with the city I lived in. And did I mention there was never any homework?

Thank you for giving me the chance to share with you most of what I've learned about being a real reporter in TV news. I hope you've learned something you didn't know before. I sincerely want you to succeed in this business that seems to change so quickly every year. The one thing that doesn't change, though, is news that is accurate, clear, honest, and told by people who are comfortable enough to be themselves will always be in demand.

If you've found this book helpful (or even if not) reach out. I'd love to hear from you.

And remember, it's only TV news.

MY GLOSSARY

A-BLOCK
The first segment of a newscast. Usually, the most important. An hour newscast will usually have six or seven blocks.

AGENDA
The motives of those you interview; what they want you to think and how they want the story to turn out.

ANCHOR

The people who usually sit at the desk and anchor the newscast.

ATTRIBUTION

One of the most important elements of a news story. The process of making clear who told you the information that you are now relaying to your audience.

B-ROLL

Video needed to cover words that you will write; doesn't usually include important sounds such as your reporter track or interviews.

BIG J

Big journalism. The feeling by some that journalism is sacred and ethics and traditional rules are unbendable.

BREAKING NEWS

Important news that is happening now. Stations will drop everything to cover it and get it on the air as soon as possible.

BROADCAST JOURNALISM

The art of telling important stories with words, video, and interviews in a simple, interesting, and understandable way.

CANDID

Someone being themselves, not being phony, letting you see what they really think and feel.

CLEARANCE FORMS

Forms crafted by television lawyers to protect from copyright infringement. Journalists need to get those forms signed by anyone who provides video to them and should credit those sources on the air to be transparent about where the video came from.

COLD OPEN

Preproduced open to a newscast containing teasable elements of the stories viewers are about to see.

CORPORATE FLACK

Company spokesperson trained to speak with the media while protecting the company they work for.

DAYSIDE

Coveted work shift that usually includes the hours from 9:00 a.m. or 10:00 a.m. to 6 p.m.

DEVELOPING STORY

Story that is a step below breaking news in intensity; something happening or something that has just changed but not as urgent; usually an update to a story the station has already been following.

EARLY MORNINGS

This shift usually begins at 4:00 a.m. and ends around 12:30 p.m. Expect to do a lot of live shots for the morning news shows.

EOS NOTE

End-of-shift note should be sent out to the staff to update them on contacts you made from your story and any follow-ups for later crews.

FACT

Something that can be proven with documentation.

GENERAL ASSIGNMENT (GA)

These reporters/MMJs don't work solely on specialties such as medicine, sports, or investigations. They are open to work on any story that comes up.

GRAPHICS

Artwork including graphs, maps, lists, bullet points, etc. (made by you or someone back at the station) that can help tell your story. If they are complicated, it's imperative to communicate as early as possible because it takes time to create graphics.

HEADLINES

Similar to cold open but may be three voice-overs read live by the anchors and not preproduced.

IFB

Interruptible foldback. That little translucent custom molded earpiece that you use to listen to the on-air broadcast *and* any instructions from the director or producer (used by reporters, anchors, MMJs and Secret Service agents). We used to plug the other end of the IFB into a box that carried the station's signal from the live truck or satellite truck. Now it's more typical to plug the IFB into your cell phone after you dial into a special IFB number at your station.

LIVE SHOT

An MMJ or reporter who reports in real time from the field via a digital, cell, microwave, or satellite uplink.

LOG VIDEO

The process of watching the video that was shot for your story and transcribing important soundbites and notable shots so that you can import that information into your script for writing and editing purposes.

LOOK-LIVE

Looks exactly like a live shot but is recorded and edited onto a story versus actually being a live element. Meant to give the illusion of being live. Though NEVER say you are live unless you really are.

MARKET SIZE

The population of the city and surrounding suburbs determines your station's market size or DMA (designated market area) compared to other population centers in the United States. The lower the number, the bigger the market (i.e., #1 New York, #2 Los Angeles, etc.). Market sizes frequently change as measured by the Nielsen Corporation. At the present time, there are 210 ranked markets in the country. Generally, the larger the market, the more money stations have to buy equipment and pay employees, but it's not always directly related.

MMJ

Multimedia journalist. This journalist does it all—researches, shoots, interviews, writes, edits, and sometimes even does live shots. It is multi-tasking to the extreme.

MONEY SHOT

A great shot, usually an action shot that is dramatic and helps tell the essence of the story.

MAN ON THE STREET (MOS)

An average person (not just a man) who offers their opinion on a news story.

NAT SOUND

Natural sound captured from your story location that helps provide context on what it was like out there. It is sound that is usually not contrived or from an interview but noises that occurred organically at your story.

NAT PACKAGE

A story with no reporter track. The story is told simply with interviews and natural sound from the location.

NEWS NOSE

Your journalistic instinct as a reporter/MMJ when you feel there's a story out there or your gut tells you you're not being told the whole truth by the people you interview.

NIGHTSIDE

The night shift, usually the hours of 3:00 p.m. to 11:30 p.m.

OPINION

Personal feelings about a news story or someone in a news story you cover. It's almost always best to keep your opinions out of the story and instead focus on the facts and other people's opinions.

OVERNIGHTS

This is the shift between nightside and early mornings. Work starts at 10:00 p.m. and goes until 6:00 a.m. or 7:00 a.m. Few reporters or MMJs work this shift. It is usually left up to producers and editors.

PACKAGE

This is the typical format of the story a reporter or MMJ will work on for the day. A package is a self-contained, edited story that usually includes soundbites, reporter tracks, a stand-up, natural sound, etc. An anchor would toss to this story. Typical length is 1:15 to 2:15, but it depends on the content.

PUBLIC INFORMATION OFFICER (PIO)

This is a person paid by a public organization, such as a fire department, police department, city, county, or federal jurisdiction. They are trained to work with the media and will be your point person to arrange interviews or give official statements after large or breaking events. Remember, they are paid by their organizations to make them look good, so they may not always be forthcoming or candid with you. But since they are paid by tax dollars, they should never lie to you. Keep in mind your emails, texts, and other communication with them can be made public if another media organization or the public asks for their records. Your written correspondence should be something you wouldn't mind the world seeing.

PERSON ON THE STREET (POS)

See Man on the Street.

PRESS CONFERENCE

A meeting called to make an announcement to all media at once. A press conference can be held by both private and public organizations. They are usually mundane and not very interesting, but there is sometimes good information that you can use from these to create your own, more visual story, outside of the meeting.

PRODUCER
Architect of the newscast; determines newscast content, story length and order, makes or orders graphics, works with the assignment desk to make sure most interesting stories are being covered, and writes most or all of the show.

"REAL" PEOPLE
Neighbors, shoppers, drivers, etc. People in the community who are not obligated to speak to you or set up for a formal interview. They offer, sometimes, the greatest insight and most interesting interviews for your stories.

REPORTER
Someone who goes out into the world, learns about something interesting, and then tells an audience about it in a way that's interesting and understandable. We know there is much more to that, but at the heart of it, we're just gatherers and tellers of stories.

RIDE-ALONG
A chance for you to spend the day with a local professional so you can see what their job entails—police officers, firefighters, paramedics, power company workers, postal carriers, etc. Riding along in the car or truck offers an interesting setting for interviews, and always results in video filled with action.

SLANT

The biased approach of the story as you undertake it. It's your goal, to remove your bias or slant and instead, tell us the story as it really is, and not perhaps, what you originally thought it would be.

Sometimes slant can have a more unbiased definition meaning the angle of your story. For instance, if you want to do a story on a hospital emergency room, your slant or angle might be seeing the ER from the perspective of a patient in the waiting room.

STAND-UP

The part of the story where the reporter is on camera speaking about something. It allows the audience to relate to the reporter instead of only hearing a voice. The best stand-ups are when you can show viewers something or take us by the hand and lead us somewhere.

TAG

Usually, a one- or two-sentence element that buttons up a story. It can give sources for viewers to learn more or know what happens next in the process. Ex. "The suspect is due back in court on August tenth where he'll be asked to enter a plea."

TEASES

Short one- or two-sentence elements in a newscast to entice viewers to keep watching so they can see what's next.

TONE

The reporter/MMJ's tone should match the story. Ex. If it's a very sad story, the reporter/MMJ should have a somber, serious tone. If it's a story about water slide day at the local theme park, the reporter/

MMJ should sound happy or energetic. Most of the time this is just common sense. However, sometimes we fail to completely match the tone of the story and our treatment of the story may come off as offensive or disrespectful. When in doubt, be serious.

TRACK

Usually refers to the voice track that an anchor, reporter, or MMJ records that is edited onto a story (also includes interview track and natural sound track).

TURNING A STORY

Going out and successfully producing a story that makes air.

UPLOAD

Transferring a digital copy of the story to the station so they can play it back on air; can be done via microwave, satellite link, or simply uploading a file from a computer to a folder back at the station. You must allow time for this upload to take place.

VET

Investigating a story tip or a source to make sure it's legitimate.

VOICEOVER (VO)

Voice over video; video is edited with the intention that an anchor or reporter/MMJ will narrate a live script (not prerecorded) while viewers see that video; usually twenty to thirty-five seconds in length.

VO/SOT

Voiceover/sound on tape; same as a VO except includes a soundbite; average length is forty seconds to one minute in length.

STATION MISSION

This is a place for you to write notes on your station mission, priorities, and philosophy. What are the kinds of stories your station wants to cover and own in the market? Ask your managers, and then write what they tell you in your own words. You can constantly refer to this page when you're looking for story ideas or angles to cover. Make sure to keep this up to date as management changes or as you move from job to job.

NOTES

This is a space to write any notes you learn as you work in this business.

_____

_____

_____

_____

_____

_____

_____

_____

_____

_____

_____

_____

_____

FOR FURTHER INFORMATION

If you're a student or professional interested in formal coaching, please email me or head to my website.

I am very interested in helping clients one-on-one or assisting news stations/organizations improve their storytelling and job satisfaction.

I am also available for in-depth lectures on the various topics found in this book.

Wayne Garcia
WayneGarciaTV@gmail.com
www.waynegarcia.tv